So now who do we vote for?

John Harris is a writer and journalist, and a former member of the Labour Party. His work appears regularly in the *Guardian* and *Observer*, and he is the author of *The Last Party*, the acclaimed pop-cultural history of the 1990s. For more information, visit www.johnharris.me.uk.

John Harris

So now who do we vote for?

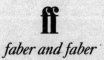

faber and faber

First published in 2005
by Faber and Faber Limited
3 Queen Square London WC1N 3AU

Typeset by Faber and Faber Limited
Printed in England by Mackays of Chatham plc, Chatham, Kent

A CIP record for this book
is available from the British Library

ISBN 0-571-22422-9

10 9 8 7 6 5 4 3 2 1

John Harris

So now who do we vote for?

faber and faber

First published in 2005
by Faber and Faber Limited
3 Queen Square London WC1N 3AU

Typeset by Faber and Faber Limited
Printed in England by Mackays of Chatham plc, Chatham, Kent

A CIP record for this book
is available from the British Library

ISBN 0–571–22422–9

10 9 8 7 6 5 4 3 2 1

For Ginny, and a politics of the heart

When the axe came into the woods, the trees all said,
'Well, at least the handle is one of us.'

Turkish folk proverb

Contents

Introduction, 1

1 The Liberal Democrats, 21
2 Hospitals, 44
3 The Labour Party, 59
4 Schools, 91
5 The Great Beyond, 119
      The SNP, 122
      Plaid Cymru, 128
      The Green Party, 133
      The Respect Coalition, 139
6 So now who do we vote for?, 151

Appendix: Labour Rebels, 165
Acknowledgements, 171

Introduction

'Sensible views and sensible arguments'

One morning in 1985, I came down to breakfast to find a Labour Party membership form sitting next to my cereal bowl. I had just turned fifteen, which marked the point at which I could formally pledge allegiance to parliamentary socialism; not wasting any time, my dad showed me where to sign and asked for my subs. I didn't mind at all: what with Thatcherism at its peak, most of the musicians I was besotted with expressing endless dissent, and the effects of what might be termed a Labour upbringing, I was only too happy to get involved. In our house, the Labour Party was like Church; what happened that morning surely amounted to the equivalent of confirmation.

I was brought up in Wilmslow, the comfortably affluent Cheshire dormitory town that lies at the southerly tip of Manchester's suburban sprawl, and forms around a third of the constituency of Tatton. Solidly and seemingly eternally Tory (our local MP was the not-yet-infamous Neil Hamilton), it was the kind of place where Conservatism was regularly warped into the most proudly reactionary beliefs. I briefly had a Saturday job in a local greengrocer's, where one morning a man breezily asked me which of the fruit on sale was South African. The consumer boycott was the last thing on his mind: he proceeded to fill two large baskets full of Outspan oranges and Cape grapes, and coolly informed everyone within earshot that 'the white people were there first'.

Undeterred by the town's crypto-fascists, I became an adolescent Labour activist. Though precious few locals ever responded positively, I dutifully delivered election leaflets through Wilmslow's letterboxes. Each month, I would turn up at a community centre in nearby Knutsford, accompanying my dad to meetings of the Tatton Constituency Party's General Management Committee, where we would sip vending-machine tea, try and forget about the overwhelming smell of cheap disinfectant and pass resolutions about dangerous local roads and insufficient bus stops, before going on to formulate motions threatening the reversal of most of the evils perpetrated by the Thatcher government.

I also set about forming a local offshoot of the Labour Party Young Socialists, then in the grip of devotees of the weekly newspaper and clandestine organisation known as Militant. Soon enough, a gaggle of them attached themselves to our branch. At first, they affected a comradely bonhomie, but their approach to other members of the party soon became clear: either you were in favour of the nationalisation of 'the top 200 companies', comprehensive workers' democracy and everyone getting paid the average wage, or you were little better than a Thatcherite. I fervently believed – and still do – in such timid notions as a progressive taxation system, a mixed economy, unilateral nuclear disarmament and comprehensive education, so they quickly made my life a nightmare. By the end of 1986, I had stepped away from the Young Socialists, and fallen back to the odd leaflet delivery.

That continued up until the 1987 election campaign, during which I finally surmised that Wilmslow was a lost cause, and put in twice-weekly canvassing rounds in the South Mancunian constituency of Davyhulme, a seat held by the grandson of Winston Churchill (who, conveniently, was his namesake). Though the statistics were against us, I had managed to work myself into a frenzy of expectant excitement, and convince myself that it might turn out to be a marginal. In reality, the prospect of a Labour win was no more likely than Neil Kinnock striding into Downing Street. Labour benefited from a 3.6 per cent swing, leaving Mr Churchill a mere 16 percentage points in front. By then, beer taps and Mancunian nightclubs were calling me away from political activism; in the wake of the 1987 defeat, I went off to university, failed to renew my membership, and restricted myself to the kind of political activity that involved righteously shouting at my friends in the pub.

What remained was a devotion to the party that was hard-wired into my subconscious, made obvious on the occasions when I entered a polling booth. Aside from the sensation of wanting a cigarette, I have never known a feeling like it: trying to use one's rational faculties, but finding them overridden by the most Pavlovian kind of reflex. There was never any question of coolly scanning the options, weighing up the parties' respective standpoints, and then mathematically making my decision. I voted Labour. Of course. That was who I was. *Labour, Labour, Labour*, as one of the politicians who features in this book would have it.

For as long as Neil Kinnock was in charge, it wasn't much of a problem. John Smith, similarly, gave me the feeling that, even if I were able to employ the thinking part of my brain, he would instantly get my vote. And even if the Clause 4-torching, market-embracing ascent of Tony Blair sowed feelings of disquiet, the dizzying probability of victory was enough to keep me happily

3

on board. Come the 1997 election, I did not just vote, either: stirred by the chance to contribute to what would surely be an epochal Labour triumph, I accompanied old Labour Party friends to the marginal constituency of Warrington South – narrowly grabbed by Labour in 1992 – and ran a day-long canvassing operation that played its own small role in securing the seat on an 11.4 per cent swing. That night, even Wilmslow decided that it had had enough: watching Martin Bell win Tatton from Neil Hamilton, I was actually reduced to tears.

Back in London, I was now the editor of *Select*, a music magazine integrally tied to the pop-cultural wave – crystallised by the post-election visit of Oasis's Noel Gallagher to Downing Street – on which Mr Blair had so shamelessly surfed. Soon after the '97 election, so giddy was I with the thrill of the Labour landslide (their overall parliamentary majority, let us not forget, was 179) that I decided to include a double-page image of Mr Blair in the magazine's monthly pull-out picture supplement. Now, the memory fills me with a shivering embarrassment. At the time, we did not receive a single letter of complaint.

Four years later came the forgotten General Election of 2001. The campaign hardly amounted to the kind of democratic carnival beloved of political enthusiasts: an era-defining clash of ideas, strewn with gaffes and unforeseen mishaps, in which the poll ratings twitched up and down and those who decided to vote approached the ballot box with a giddy sense of anticipation. Nothing much happened, though the odd image should stir the requisite memories: the Labour Party poster in which Margaret Thatcher's hairdo had been Photoshopped onto William Hague's face; Mr Blair being ambushed by Sharon

Storer, a Birmingham woman whose cancer-suffering husband had allegedly been denied a bed at the city's Queen Elizabeth Hospital; the occasion when, seeking to bring some of New Labour's good cheer to North Wales, John Prescott let fly at an egg-hurling protester with an admirably instinctive left hook.

Most of the excitement was sucked from the campaign by the fact that, as the press announced well in advance ('Blair's 227 Majority', predicted the ever-reliable *Sun*, well over a month before polling day), another Labour landslide was never seriously in doubt. And so it turned out: the Conservatives advanced by one seat, Labour and the Liberal Democrats lost and gained six respectively, William Hague valiantly called it quits, and Mr Blair smiled yet another of his invincible smiles. How many hopeful TV viewers watched David Dimbleby and Peter Snow attempting to inject the results with some kind of drama, only to surmise that politics suddenly didn't seem to matter and crawl off to bed? Four years before, charged up with the excitement of breathing non-Tory air, I had reluctantly turned in as the sun came up; in 2001, puzzled by the tedium of it all, I was asleep by 1 a.m.

The government, of course, had no option but to hail the result as a solid approval of the New Labour project. Mr Blair spoke of a 'remarkable and historic victory, a mandate for reform and for investment in the future'. Two years later, one government minister stoutly claimed that 'the campaign revealed the deep fault-lines in British politics, and gave us a clear indication that most people supported Labour's ambitions for the public services'. What had actually happened was surely a little more equivocal: far from sprinting to the polls in a frenzy of Blairite excitement, millions of those of who had voted Labour in 1997 had taken account of the country's economic stability, stolen one horrified glance at the Tories, and apathetically put a cross in the Labour box. Though reaching solid conclusions in the ambiguous world of election results is a game probably best left to brassnecked politicians, the result seemed to amount to a shrug: if the people spoke, they said something like, 'Oh, go on then.'

However, if all that suggests a strange kind of indifferent endorsement, for one group of voters the prospect of a visit to the ballot box was a little more troubling. For those of us who had stuck with the Labour Party through the dread days of the 1980s, the first New Labour term contained plenty to worry about. The items on the list now have the ring of political cliché, though they're worth recounting: the cutting of single-parent and incapacity benefit, the introduction of student tuition fees, craven joining-in with the American bombing of Iraq in December 1998 (which neatly synchronised with the peak of the Lewinsky scandal), Jack Straw's attempts to end the right to trial by jury, and the control-freakery whereby Ken Livingstone was denied the chance to run as Labour's candidate for London Mayor, and Rhodri Morgan was initially sidelined as the party's leader in Wales.

Worse still, though the press and broadcast media left them strangely obscured, moves were being made on the public services that, had the Tories enacted them, would have made even the most moderate Labour activist grind their teeth in anger. As early as 1998, the government reversed its old opposition to the use of the Private Finance Initiative to build and run hospitals, thus allowing such firms as Jarvis and Amec to extend their tentacles into the health service, and thousands of hapless support staff to be nudged into the private sector. At the launch of

Labour's 2001 education manifesto, Mr Blair talked enthusiastically about state schools being run by private companies, having already approved the new idea of Local Education Authorities handing over their functions to the private sector.

If anyone of a progressive disposition could be expected to feel queasy about large swathes of the government's record, there were frequent occasions when the government affected to arrogantly scoff at our objections. No matter that we were their natural supporters: so keen were they to send out the right signals to their new ex-Thatcherite friends that the Labour Party's old bond with its core constituency seemed to count for very little. In July 1999, Mr Blair told an audience of venture capitalists that his experience of dealing with public sector workers had left him with 'scars on my back after two years in government. And heaven knows what it will be like after a bit longer.' In 2000, as opposition to his draconian tendencies reached a crescendo, Mr Straw launched his infamous attack on 'woolly minded Hampstead liberals'.

Not long after, I shared a BBC studio with Sîon Simon, the creepily Blairite MP for Birmingham Erdington and sometime *News of the World* columnist, who spent much of his time making dismissive asides about the allegedly absurd views of *Guardian* readers. In response, I irately asked him a handful of questions: Who stuffed the Labour Party's election envelopes? Who canvassed the estates? Who could be relied upon to vote Labour in just about any eventuality? As 2001 approached, it seemed more than a little counter-intuitive to vote for a government that was in the habit of sneering at me.

And yet, and yet. For all my misgivings, at least some of the government's record gave cause for qualified support.

Occasionally, when faced with the right kind of audience, Mr Blair would lay claim to it all, as happened at the 1999 Labour Conference. His boasts ran as follows: 'All employees with the right to a paid holiday. Leave for parents to take time off work for a family crisis. The right for union members to have their union recognized. Maternity grant doubled . . . Seven million families with the largest ever rise in Child Benefit Britain has seen.' (According to one apocryphal Labour Party story, after each achievement, a stoic Gordon Brown quietly turned to the person next to him and whispered, 'He opposed that.')

There was also the minimum wage, the Working Families Tax Credit, and – most important of all – the beginnings of increased investment in education and health. Even a journalist happily trapped in the London media bubble did not have to look far for corroborating evidence: thanks to Mr Brown's largesse, my cousin, a working single mother, had seen her income rise by £50 a week; my mum, a teacher in Mancunian sixth-form college, said that she and her colleagues were at last starting to see the fruits of increased funding.

Overarching all that, meanwhile, was the glorious pleasure of seeing the Tories kicked to the political sidelines. After eighteen years of political torment, it would surely be little short of infantile to switch allegiance after a mere 48 months. As evidenced by the low turnout in Labour's heartlands – which contributed to a measly nationwide figure of 59.4 per cent – some erstwhile Labour voters stopped short of voting for another party and simply sat on their hands. People like me, for better or worse, swallowed our misgivings and stuck with them.

By 2001, my old Pavlovian instincts had faded, Still, I certainly wasn't going to vote Conservative. Switching to the Greens or the newly-founded Socialist Alliance seemed to be not only a waste, but – certainly in the case of the latter – a lurch back into the company of the kind of people who had contributed to making the Thatcher years such a misery. The Liberal Democrats, easily the most tempting receptacle for a protest vote, affected to oppose the government while apparently not knowing quite why. 'Freedom, Justice, Honesty: these sum up what the Liberal Democrats stand for,' their manifesto bravely announced; they hardly seemed to represent a thoroughgoing alternative.

So, shaking off a mixture of guilt, mild bafflement and creeping anxiety, I did it. Later that night, millions dozed off, Mr Blair smiled, and Labour's second term began. Not long after, those two planes ploughed into the New York skyline, and the Bush administration decided to turn its sights on Iraq. Meanwhile, what with Foundation Hospitals, top-up fees and yet more PFI projects, the advocates of the New Labour project who seemed to take grinning delight in their trashing of the party's old orthodoxy were freshly emboldened. Soon enough, David Blunkett managed to ooze even more contempt for woolly liberals than his predecessor.

The last four years have thus been contorted, topsy-turvy and politically exasperating. By their midway point, countless Labour supporters had surely reached the same kind of conclusion. We didn't want the world. We understood the need for caution and compromise. But really: what was all *this*?

At the time of writing, it looks like an election in 2005 might have roughly the same contours as the one that took place in 2001. As far as the Tory–Labour battle is concerned, we seem set for a campaign at least partly based on the bugbears of the tabloid press – immigration, Brussels bureaucrats, allegedly rampant criminals – coupled with an ossified debate about whose 'reform' proposals might best improve the public services. These days, that argument is rarely a matter of two competing visions of society; if you want a flavour of the forthcoming battle, think back to the summer of 2004 and the strange bidding war focused on whether Oliver Letwin or Gordon Brown would sack the most civil servants.

Thankfully, there looks likely to be another axis of argument, built around droves of disaffected Labour supporters, and one issue in particular. It is not the purpose of this book to hack through the tangled history of Blair's misadventure in Iraq – but some crucial points demand to be made.

The first transcends party politics, and relates to the workings of our imperfect democracy – and though it is not a contention uniquely bound up with elections, its truth is often proven via the ballot box. It's an old-fashioned idea, but if political systems are to remain healthy, they depend on mechanisms that work to occasionally restore a kind of equilibrium. If a government gravely screws up, it has to be held to account – not merely in terms of being questioned and scrutinised, but either being seen to jettison the relevant personnel, or suffering a blow at the hands of the electorate. Anthony Eden resigned after the Suez crisis, and Mrs Thatcher was fatally weakened by the Poll Tax. James Callaghan was defeated after the Winter of Discontent; John Major's demise can be traced to his government's bungling of the European Exchange Rate Mechanism. If the detached, cosseted reality of our system of government often seems to fly in the face of the kind of ideas studied by political science undergraduates – the Contract between Government and

Governed, the Execution of the Popular Will – these kind of episodes suggest that, when necessary, the right correctional processes can still kick in.

Thus far, Mr Blair has lived in happy denial of all that, and the toxic effects on our political system – as evidenced by endless talk about a breakdown of trust – are clear enough. Without betraying a contempt for democratic politics, you can't take a country to war on a false prospectus, bolstered by your own hardening of sketchy intelligence into certain fact, and then blithely insist that everyone should accept you acted in 'good faith' and shut up about it.

Moreover, the pro-war faction's endless trumpeting of the fall of Saddam and their idiotically rhetorical question to those who were opposed – Do you want him back? – hardly nullify the sense of a monumental set of errors. If Bush and Blair's state-craft led to the future of Iraq being whittled down to a choice between Ba'athist dictatorship and blood-splattered anarchy, then the accusation of howling political failure still sticks, a fact only underlined by their lamentable neglect of the Middle East peace process.

Quite apart from the idea of calling Mr Blair to account, Iraq needs to make an impact on the next election for one other reason. On that chilly afternoon in February 2003 when a million-plus people marched through London, one got the sense of a worrying schism between Westminster politics and the opinions of the people our MPs claim to represent. A majority of Britons were opposed to military action, and yet government and opposition were united by a staunch belligerence (indeed, Iain Duncan Smith seemed yet more keen on the idea of war than Mr Blair). Even when Charles Kennedy eventually decided to tumble off the fence and address the anti-war multitudes in Hyde Park, his vocabulary hardly suggested a mind in tune with the mood of at least half the electorate: 'I have yet to be persuaded that the case for war against Iraq has been made,' he said, to a smattering of understandably limp applause.

An election might provide a belated opportunity for all that anger about Iraq to find a productive outlet: backing the Lib Dems, for all their hesitancy, might send out the right kind of signal; as would support for Plaid Cymru or the SNP, or – for those of a slightly more uncompromising mindset – the Greens or George Galloway's Respect Coalition. His eternal desire to 'move on' notwithstanding, Mr Blair may well deserve nothing else; not just in terms of a shock for the Labour Party on election day, but an ongoing re-routing of the campaign away from the agenda put forward by the government – and, in all likelihood, the Tories – towards the most murky aspect of Mr Blair's premiership.

All that said, as outrage over Iraq has simmered on, there has been a strange sense of that anger turning myopic and actually beginning to work in the government's favour. New Labour's cheerleaders are prone to characterise just about all opposition to the Blair government as solely Iraq-related, as if their detractors have no other grounds for hostility; on occasion, a perfectly reasonable desire to pursue the subject until Blair is forced to apologise or resign (or both) seems to prove their point. As 2004 rolled on, the Prime Minister's refusal to cede any ground on Iraq started to suggest that his opponents were wasting their breath; moreover, in the flurry of Hutton and Butler, Abu Ghraib and Fallujah, the worrying aspects of all kinds of other policies were perhaps being neglected by the government's opponents.

The public, New Labour recurrently claims, is much more interested in schools and hospitals. Fine: on that score, there are plenty of stories that suggest that Iraq may not be the only reason to think about taking your vote elsewhere.

During the 1980s and beyond, those who spent their spare time decrying the Conservative government devoted a great deal of their anger to the totemic Tory policy of privatisation. As far as public opinion was concerned, they often seemed to be shouting into the void: in the face of Mrs Thatcher's seductive vision of popular share ownership, and all those entreaties to tell Sid, such trifles as the knock-down prices at which the UK's utilities were auctioned seemed to count for very little. Even the venerable Harold Macmillian, gravely warning about the selling-off of the family silver, was ignored. Only towards the end of Britain's garage sale, with the offloading of electricity, water and the railways, did any sense of public disquiet start to bubble up.

Right up until the 1997 election, the Conservatives' fondness for handing chunks of the public sector to private interests was a recurrent source of irate Labour complaint. In 1993, John Prescott assured his party that, upon the return of a Labour government, the railways would be 'quickly and effectively dealt with, and returned to public ownership'. Even after the ascent of Mr Blair, the party's tone remained one of almost moral outrage. At the 1996 party conference, the shadow transport secretary Andrew Smith took aim at the Tory proposal to privatise air traffic control: 'Our air is not for sale,' he thundered. The same year, taking issue with the Conservatives' proposed use of the Private Finance Initiative in the NHS, Harriet Harman – then a front-bench Labour health spokeswoman – was moved to claim that

'When the private sector is building, owning, managing and running a hospital, that hospital has been privatised.' This, we were obviously meant to think, was a very bad thing indeed.

In government – and particularly during its second term – New Labour has dispensed with all of that, extending privatisation into areas the Party once passionately fought to keep off-limits: most notably, the public's beloved schools and hospitals. Perhaps mindful of the fact that opinion polls recurrently show a handsome majority of Britons – sometimes as high as over 80 per cent – opposed to private involvement in public services, the government rarely uses the P-word. Large swathes of their policies, however, amount to the same thing: the entry of private firms into health and education, the consequent arrival of the profit motive, the cutting-loose of those areas from any recognisable kind of democratic control – and the dilution of that quaint old ideal termed the public service ethos. In the course of the research for this book, I discovered as much during encounters with trade union members, healthworkers and teachers, and admirably brave local activists who were attempting to stem the privatisation tide.

As far as schools are concerned, New Labour began with the policy termed LEA Outsourcing, whereby several English Local Education Authorities had their functions transferred to private companies, the vast majority of whom singularly failed to pull off the envisaged educational miracles. In the wake of that policy came the City Academies initiative, which offered private benefactors effective control of a raft of new schools in exchange for a relatively trifling contribution of £2 million. Among the first to sign up were a London sports agent, the chairman of Saga Holidays, and – most controversially – a Christian fundamentalist car dealer named Peter Vardy, keen on the notion of according the theory of creationism the same importance as Darwinian evolution. Thus far, he runs two state schools in the North East, with a third to follow. Mr Blair thinks highly of him: 'I know there are a lot of criticisms of those schools,' he said on *Newsnight* in 2002, 'but look at the results. Most parents want their children to have results as good as that.'

Underpinning a great deal of New Labour's embrace of privatisation is the Private Finance Initiative. PFI occasionally surfaces in the liberal press, but usually seems too labyrinthine an issue to merit a place on the front page. At its core, however, is a simple enough idea: rather than government coming up with the money for new hospitals and schools, the private sector borrows the funds on the open market, builds the wards and classrooms, and then leases them back to the state for a period stretching into the far distance. In addition, private firms see to such so-called ancillary services as cleaning, catering and security. As I found out during a visit to the first ever PFI hospital, experience suggests an in-built drive to cut costs and thereby maximise financial returns: money that would, if the schemes were kept public, go on patient care and education.

Finally, there are Foundation Hospitals: another one of those innocuous sounding initiatives that actually denotes something altogether more sinister. The idea is to honour high-performing hospitals by cutting them loose from the NHS, obliging them to make an annual surplus for reinvestment, and leaving them free to borrow their own money for new projects and use the services of private companies. Government rhetoric claims that they will be nominally owned by mixture of staff, patients and the local public – though the legislation that brought them into being allows for a slightly more unpalatable arrangement. In the words of one health expert, 'The bill allows any private-sector body – from Bupa to Boots – to apply to be a foundation trust and run NHS services.' Of late, overseas healthcare companies have been setting up shop in the UK, preparing to enter the hitherto fenced-off NHS. Two of the most powerful are the American firms Kaiser Permanente and United Health. It's a fair bet that you'll be hearing more of them in future.

Even without that eventuality, Foundation Hospitals – to be joined, according to policies for Labour's third term floated last summer, by up to a thousand equally independent Foundation Schools – are emblematic of one of New Labour's more noxious articles of faith: the idea that setting public institutions into competition with one another is the best way of raising standards. All this seems to be leading to the kind of world that the Labour Party once set itself against: a very modern dystopia of franchising, two-tier public services – what, after all, will become of the hospital denied foundation status, or the school down the road from the City Academy? – and privilege masquerading as choice.

What's strange is that the breaking-up and selling-off of the public sector so rarely intrudes on mainstream politics. The Tories and the Labour Party usually seem locked in a debate about each other's market-tilted designs. Dissidents on the government's side might occasionally wrest the odd concession, but the prevailing direction remains the same. The Liberal Democrats, meanwhile, profess to be 'sceptical' about certain schemes, and go as far as publicly opposing some of them, but won't go near the kind of solid, first-principle commitments that millions of people would surely like to hear. Very often, it feels as if the Westminster class has largely made up its mind, and those of us who don't agree are left hobbling towards the political fringes.

There are those who would respond with impatience to the kind of concerns outlined above, point to other aspects of the government's record, and claim that such worries are thereby either counterbalanced or reduced to the level of nitpicking. And of course, relative to the doom-laden days of Conservative government, things are better. The kind of first-term policies alluded to above back up the point. The government's record on primary and nursery education only serves to underline it. There has been large investment in schools and hospitals; the renewed presence of those two words at the centre of political debate is often held up as proof of the government's success.

But having progressive – oh, go on then, *socialist* – politics is not just a matter of wishing to see more new schools and hospitals per se; its is also bound up with the question of what *kind* of schools and hospitals you want. Sticking to those kind of beliefs should also lead to worry about a generation of students who will finish their education with an astronomical debt – a debt that, if they gained a place at a particularly prestigious university, will be all the higher. It should give rise to instinctive alarm about a Home Secretary given to legitimising ghoulish scare-mongering about refugees and aspiring to the creation of a society 'in which people feel free to be able to express sensible views and have sensible arguments'; anxiety about a Labour Prime Minister who seemed to luxuriate in his role as George W. Bush's most treasured PR prop; and exasperation with a government which has shirked from the idea that, if Britain is to have truly dependable public services, its wealthier residents will have to pay proportionally more tax.

What often most concerns those opponents of New Labour with some residual attachment to the Labour Party is the vexing question of its future. Its alleged rising stars seem to be Blairite apparatchiks, coolly skilled at the practice of power, but lacking when it comes to any sense of left-leaning conviction. On the backbenches, there lurks a handful of political braggarts who delight in opposition to Labour's traditions. Who, for example, could have not felt queasy at the sight of Sîon Simon taking to his feet in the first Prime Minister's Questions after the Hutton Report and gleefully wondering whether now was the time to privatise the BBC?

Disquiet within the party has obviously done its work: Labour membership is currently at half its 1997 level, and some of its more forward-thinking figures have been to heard to wonder whether the eventual snuffing-out of Blairism might leave them with a moribund husk that was impossible to revive. In that sense, it may well be necessary to administer a cruel kindness and temporarily desert the Labour Party so as to shock it back to life. The seeming impossibility of a Conservative victory perhaps creates space for exactly that kind of tactic; there again, a Michael Howard government may perhaps be too nightmarish a prospect for a lot of people to dice with.

This book was written in the midst of volatile political weather. Many of the encounters with politicians on which it is built took place through the spring and summer of 2004, when the prospect of a war-battered Tony Blair leaving Downing Street was often alleged to be imminent, the *Guardian* was excitedly running G2 cover stories about a forthcoming Brown premiership, and the old idea of voting Labour with a sense of optimism seemed to be on the verge of restoration. I often felt sceptical about the notion of the Chancellor moving into Number 10 and neutralising Blairism's most malign aspects, but the prospect of his leadership was enough to make me think seriously about returning to the Labour fold. Such was the message of a number of the senior Labour dissidents who gave me their time: Hold on. Don't worry so much. Things, as someone once sang, can only get better.

By the high summer, however, Mr Blair had triumphantly exited the debate on the Butler Report, flown off on a grand tour that would culminate in a stay with Silvio Berlusconi, and served apparent notice of his continued invincibility. The subsequent announcement that he expected to depart Downing Street some time between 2008 and 2009 might have given some succour to dismayed ex-Labour supporters – but it still begged all kinds of questions. Why did we have to wait that long? In the meantime, wouldn't the cabal of Blairites at the top of the party seek to tighten their grip, even trying to pull off the seemingly impossible by appointing the dreaded Alan Milburn as the Prime-Minister-in-waiting? And what if the retirement promise went the way of Mr Blair's rumoured guarantees to the Chancellor and was eventually forgotten?

One possible consequence of the news seemed particularly grim. In its wake, someone described as 'one of Blair's associates' raved to a *New Statesman* journalist about the Prime Minister's new chance of complete political freedom. 'We've never had this opportunity before,' they said. 'He can act without the need for alliances or deals. It's a liberating feeling. He won't have to worry about getting re-elected. We can take more risks.'

Such, it seemed, was the crystallisation of a glib contempt – not only for the debate within the Labour Party, but for the checks and balances of our democracy. Even with Labour's dissidents occasionally acting up and the distant prospect of electoral failure, we still got Iraq, Foundation Hospitals, tuition fees and privatisation extended into hitherto virgin territory. Without such constraints, who knows where we might be taken?

Thus, even in the context of Mr Blair's alleged timetable for retirement, the prospect of voting Labour is still couched in dread. And so the question presents itself anew: So *now* who do we vote for?

1 The Liberal Democrats

'When I get cross, I get cross, and I say so.'

Among dejected Labour supporters, one line of conversation occurs more often than most. It usually signals either a desperate wish to send Mr Blair an unmistakable message, or – and here, it often comes wrapped in a noticeable smugness – a belief that politics has shifted off the left/right axis of yore, history is no longer a useful foundation for one's political loyalties, and it's time that progressive people forgot about such trifles as Lloyd George's antipathy to the trade unions and the treachery of the SDP, and grasped a new set of realities. Who hasn't heard the words, uttered like some statement of revolutionary intent, 'This time, I'm voting Liberal Democrat'?

Of course, doing so involves a more convoluted set of considerations than tends to apply to a party who are ready to become the government. For a start, voting Lib Dem means bravely ignoring the warnings that you might accidentally contribute to an unexpected triumph for the Tories. If the electoral arithmetic seems to suggest that a Tory win in 2005 is pretty much impossible, the government is still well aware of the terrifying nature of the argument: as a rattled Peter Hain put it in June last year, 'These people who think they can get a free hit will find themselves with a rude shock and a Tory MP. They could deprive us of our majority. It isn't teaching us a lesson or giving us a message. What's it's doing is bringing in Michael Howard by the back door.' Like a cracking whip, such words are often enough to rein in even the most irate Labour supporter.

Still, if you can resist the call to get back in line, the pro-Lib Dem argument perhaps goes something like this. To vote for the third party is to voice your dissent on such issues as Iraq and tuition fees. More grandly, it suggests that you aspire to the centre of gravity of British politics being pulled away from the malign knot that seems to tie together both Conservative and Labour Parties: string-'em-up illiberalism, the endlessly disingenuous idea that public services can be improved without big changes in income tax, an unchanging belief in the electoral system that may well lie at the heart of the problem. A big enough showing for the Liberal Democrats might threaten some of this by bringing them into a Labour-led coalition, or threatening the Tories' place as the official opposition, or crowning them as the de facto representatives of Britain's neglected progressive constituency . . . or *something*, at least.

Lately, of course, the Lib Dems have purposely placed themselves as a vessel for the votes of those who feel an ever-increasing queasiness about the Blair project – although on the issue of the war, they managed to suffuse their stance with a strange sense of equivocation, as if they were, in the words of one commentator, 'scared of doing the right thing, lest they be accused of opportunism'. Soon after the invasion of Iraq began, in one of those rather idiotic surrenders to supposed protocol that gives the political class a bad name, they suddenly muted their opposition to the invasion and announced that they were duty-bound to 'support our troops in action', seemingly in case some demoralised Tommy got wind that Charles Kennedy was still not keen and suddenly deserted his post.

And yet from time to time, they have managed to make the right kind of noises. On a few occasions, for example, Mr Kennedy has seen fit to issue uncharacteristically forthright pronouncements on the dangers of extending the claws of the private sector into the public services. 'Once you undermine the public sector ethic of people like teachers, doctors and nurses, then you change the very dynamic of what they do,' he said in the summer of 2001. 'How many people working for a private company have the same passionate commitment as those working in a public service?'

Three years later, their education spokesman, Phil Willis, contributed to the debate on the conclusive second reading of the top-up fees legislation as follows: 'I was looking forward to a principled debate, but we have had a shabby charade. Labour Member after Labour Member will line up tonight to go into the Aye lobby to support a Thatcherite policy in direct opposition to what they said during the General Election campaign, betraying the principles on which the Labour Party is built.' In Scotland, it was the presence of the Lib Dems in the ruling coalition that ensured the punitive English model of tuition fees never made it to the statute book.

Before anyone gets too carried away, however, it should be borne in mind that the last two years have seen the Lib Dems take a marked stride to the right. Their economics people express sympathy with the idea that Britain's thoroughly deregulated economy still needs to slough off allegedly stifling red tape, and stress their opposition to any above-inflation increases to the minimum wage. And despite the kind of commendably fired-up rhetoric referred to above, their occasional scepticism about the privatisation of public services often seems to be pushed to the margins. A recent policy statement opened with the claim that 'Liberal Democrats start with a bias in favour of market solutions'; when quizzed about their standpoints on such matters as the Private Finance Initiative and LEA Out-sourcing, their MPs will habitually voice that worryingly Blairite belief that whatever seems to work is worth considering.

From a charitable perspective, the caution and inconsistency of their pronouncements might be put down to their position in the shadows cast by the two main parties, and the distorting effects of our electoral system. Perhaps, goes this argument, most Liberal Democrats are intuitive left-wingers, but they're obliged to moderate their policies because the short-term key to building their success lies partly in attracting a fragile con-stituency of disaffected Tories. When I spent some time in the company of Lord Rennard, the campaigns chief alleged to be their answer to Peter Mandelson, one of his answers said it all. 'The most fundamental mistake anyone makes with Lib Dem strategy is to say, "Are you going for the Labour or the Tory vote?" It would be a mad strategy for us to say, "We just want Labour votes" or "We just want Tory votes." The only way we can make progress is if we win from both.'

Unfortunately, even without the necessity of mopping up disgruntled Conservatives, most of my encounters with Liberal Democrats suggested that their politics would always be frus-tratingly hazy. From political anoraks who had groped their way into national politics after a short lifetime fixated with the Lib Dems' beloved local issues, to those waifs and strays pulled into politics by the birth of the SDP, their conversation recur-rently betrayed the absence of any real political compass, as if the Liberal Party's replacement all those years ago as Britain's leading progressive force had left them and their allies forever lost.

If the Liberal Democrats still seem to have a hole where their philosophy should be, their leader often seems to embody the problem. This is not just a matter of his own rather vague political convictions; Charles Kennedy's fuzziness is also evident in matters of the most elementary strategy. In June last year, for example, he should surely have used the Prime Minister's Questions that followed Labour's Iraq-prompted rout in the Euro and local elections to further pressure Tony Blair about the biggest mistake of his premiership. Instead, he asked a convoluted question about the idea of taxing aeroplane fuel. That day, the usual groans from the Labour backbenches seemed less like mealy-mouthed sabotage than a deserved response to yet another fluffed shot at the most open of political goals.

I visited Mr Kennedy one Wednesday afternoon a few months before that, a couple of weeks prior to his non-appearance for Gordon Brown's budget statement, the result of which was a week of innuendo-laden whispers focused on the allegation that he was a wheezing alcoholic. I was met in the Houses of Parliament's Central Lobby by a young woman with teeth-braces. By way of small talk, I asked her where we were going. 'To meet *Charles*,' she said, as if I was about to be introduced to the future monarch.

Deposited in a two-chair reception area, I tuned into the chatter eddying from a nearby room, where a couple of twentysome-things were chewing over the forthcoming European election campaign with a grey-haired, loudly enthusiastic colleague. 'You know that Monty Python film, *Life of Brian*?' he asked them. 'Well, we should do something like that bit where they're talking about the Romans – only our thing'll say, "What has *Europe* ever done for us?"' Never let it be said that the political class knows nothing of the cultural cutting-edge.

I was eventually led up to Mr Kennedy's office, to find him wedged behind his faux-antique desk with a Silk Cut in one hand and a can of Diet Coke in the other. To his left sat his press secretary Jackie Rowley, an elegant woman dressed in a trouser suit, who nodded whenever her boss said something of which she particularly approved. Her head moved most frantically when he was tentatively outlining the party's strong base among the young. 'You hear that a lot of young people are very disaffected by politics, and yet we are finding – and have been for quite a long time now – that on a whole range of issues, there's a tremendous level of interest in what we've got to say,' he said; his words doubtless corresponded to an internal memo titled 'Young People are Liberal Democrat People', or some such.

If a lot of his replies sounded scripted, there were also hamstrung by his seeming belief that making the kind of statements that befit a political leader is a matter of couching everything in terms of measured equivocation. As a result, he often ends up sounding quite odd. The problem isn't helped by the fact that he has evident trouble ordering his thoughts, so that what he says frequently tumbles out in a soup of *ers* and *aahs*. Most of the time, in fact, he addresses the government's shortcomings with the kind of mildly confused vexation that some people get from difficult crossword clues.

And so it proved that afternoon. 'I think people want their politicians to articulate their aspirations,' he explained, by way of setting out his stall. 'People know what the problems are when they walk out of their front door in the morning, so they don't need me to go on and on about what's wrong. What they want is a much more solution-based approach to politics, specific on individual issues, and then they build up a composite picture of the kind of people you are, and whether your case stacks up. That's what we're trying to do, and it's what I'm most comfortable with. And therefore I'm not going to be changing my ways, as it were, over the next however long it is – eighteen months, or twelve months or something – till the election.'

Inevitably, we spent a lot of time talking about his approach to the issue of Iraq. Perhaps, I ventured, things had taken such an awful turn that Mr Kennedy could occasionally have moved away from his usual hesitancy: as the sense of government skulduggery deepened, and the country itself tumbled into chaos, and people from all kinds of political backgrounds felt a kind of outraged bafflement that the government (and official opposition, come to think of it) had pushed us down such a disastrous road, perhaps he could have raised his voice a bit more. He might also have been brave enough to put his disquiet in a broad political context: Mr Blair's absurdly toadying relationship with Bush, say, or the venality at the heart of the latter's administration.

By way of fleshing all this out, I took him back to a chilly afternoon in February 2003. 'When you spoke at Hyde Park, at the big march –' I began.

'Yes!' he exclaimed. '*Uh-huh.*' He sounded stagily emphatic, as if he was keen to convey a fond memory of such an important event.

Through gritted teeth, I reminded him of the soundbite – 'I have yet to be persuaded that the case for war against Iraq has been made' – that had so meekly crept on to that evening's news bulletins. What I missed there, I explained, was any sense of indignation. And a wider context: I would have liked to hear him underwrite people's anxieties about the neo-conservatives in the American government. Because I would never be 'persuaded' by George Bush and Donald Rumsfeld and Paul Wolfowitz, knowing what I do about them.

'No, no,' he nodded. 'And nor me, obviously. But the, er . . . er, I think how you choose to articulate yourself, I mean, is obviously quite a personal thing apart from anything else. Each and every one of us has our own certain style. But you do get a sense of, er . . . people do want a degree of anger, if you like, of passion, and I think that's important, and it's got its place, and, er . . . you know, when I get cross, I get cross, and I say so.'

He drew breath. 'But I think also, that you've got to be very careful. There's a dividing line between anger, which I would say – for example, with Michael Howard – just looks rather synthetic a great deal of the time, and isn't really persuading people. Because people just turn off. That just confirms many of their prejudices about politics. The result is one big slanging match, and I don't think that, as a party, we want to be in that, because I think our appeal is quite distinct. We don't have that degree of tribal loyalty, which has tended historically to attach to the other two parties. Where we're winning our loyalty from, progressively, is a much more fluid, mobile, much less deferential society that just doesn't take anything that's handed down from the top table.'

But his mistake on Iraq was surely bound up with a political flow that moved in the other direction – a groundswell of public opinion that he failed to either pre-empt or tap into. And there was more he could do on that front, wasn't there?

'Well, I think there is,' he agreed, 'and this is something that we work on in here – Jackie and myself and others – every day of the week. Yes, we do need to give a voice and a sense of hope and vision to people who are looking for something different and something better from their politics, and certainly don't feel that they're getting it from the old two parties at the moment. That has to be the objective for us; that's what we're working on. But it takes a lot of time. And you need coverage to do it. And of course, we've got to fight considerably harder for coverage, compared to the other two, who are guaranteed it.'

Unfortunately, the hole in this argument was gaping. At Hyde Park, his media exposure was assured. And even if a lack of time was an issue, he had his six seconds at the top of the news, and he fluffed them. But anyway – while we were on the subject of Iraq, by way of probing exactly where the Lib Dems were coming from, I asked him about the idea that it had been, as the slogan would have it, a war for oil. If the claim was initially associated with placard-carrying lefties, it has long since slipped into the political mainstream. By the early summer of 2004, for example, the achingly respectable John Kerry was telling the American electorate that 'We should never be sending young Americans to fight and die for oil.' Was that, I wondered, something he'd feel comfortable expressing – the idea that the war had the worst kind of ulterior motives?

'Well, I wasn't . . . I didn't think that this war was prosecuted on the basis of oil, although there may well have been . . . erm . . . er . . . interests involved in that [*sarcastic laughter*]. The, er . . . I mean, it may well, I think, have been a component in the politics and the economics of the United States, in *their* thinking . . .'

Then it *was* a crucial factor.

'Um . . . er . . . It *may* have been. But I don't think it was the fundamental one. I think the fundamental one was much more as George Bush put it at the time, you know, that this was a case of . . . well, it was all wrapped up in everything post-September 11th, everything going back to his father's presidency of the United States, really, in many ways. And therefore focusing on just the oil issue or making that the principal issue . . . although a lot of people were persuaded by that, I wasn't sufficiently persuaded by that bit of the argument myself, at the time.'

Without wanting to sound excessively churlish, the reply was absolutely hopeless: confused, contradictory, ill-informed – the kind of answer one might expect from a nervous participant in a TV Vox Pop rather than the leader of a major political party. It was his worst of the afternoon, though on a number of other subjects, things didn't get much better.

We managed a brief and rather baffling exchange about the noises being made by some of his frontbenchers about the relationship between private and public sectors. When I heard them talk about 'tough choices' in this area, I said, I heard echoes of the same New Labour approach that made me feel very queasy indeed. In fact, I began to question the idea of voting Liberal Democrat at all.

'Well,' he replied, 'we don't see any philosophical, or for that matter policy contradiction in being in favour of tough choices, which undoubtedly is what politics is about, whatever part of the spectrum you occupy. But making those tough choices to deliver more enlightened citizenship, liberal policies for the individual versus the instincts and the interests of the state, more emphasis on the environment, better quality funded and devolved public services more locally accountable . . .'

Trying to nudge the conversation towards something approaching specifics, I butted in. It worried me, I said, that he'd claimed that the Lib Dems have no 'ideological' objection to an increased relationship between the private sector and the health service and the education system.

'We don't have an *ideological* objection,' he replied, 'but we don't lose sight of the public and the community and citizen's interest along the way. You should judge each one as it comes. Um . . .'

But what about that righteous contribution to the debate he had made in 2001? 'Once you undermine the public sector ethic of people like teachers, doctors and nurses, then you change the *very dynamic* of what they do.' On that basis, how did he feel about the effect on the notion of public service when hospital porters and caterers and cleaners were transferred into the private sector? That would inevitably undermine and fracture it, wouldn't it?

'Well, it depends. I think that if you take the public sector employees, particularly maybe the more ancillary ones in the health service, as the biggest component of all this, there shouldn't be a fixed ideological view that it is absolutely beyond the pale. What you're concerned about are people's terms and conditions and motivations and self-esteem. Now, I think the problem has been, both through the Conservative years and the Labour years, so far, that there hasn't been an adequate level of rhetoric which actually communicates to people that the government doesn't just know the price of everything, but it also appreciates the value of a lot of things. And it's the absence of that that I think is the key disturbing factor, which I would hope as a party we would have a very different approach over if we were in government.'

31

What did this mean? Did even he know? As we carried on talking, I really wasn't sure. In response to a point I made about the tendency of PFI projects to create two-tier workforces, Mr Kennedy slid into an equally woolly oration about the link between decentralisation and regional variations in pay. When I quizzed him about the vague noises his party had made about snowballing corporate power and the increasingly standardised face of the average British town, he threw back a couple of sentences about increasing urban crime and made the fairly idiotic point that 'if people want a McDonalds, they should have a McDonalds'.

For all his shortcomings, however, there seemed little doubt that Charles Kennedy knew that he was on to a good thing. 'I think if I could characterise the difference between this parliament and the previous one, there were perhaps quite a lot of *disappointed* Labour voters in Tony Blair's first term, but that has turned into something much more disjointed and disaffected, not least because of Iraq,' he said, with an air of contentment. 'After six-plus years in office – seven-plus years by the time of the next election – there's just a sense that that heady optimism of 1997 has dissolved, never to re-emerge. So there's an increasing constituency of disaffected Labour voters – no question about that whatsoever.'

So, Charles Kennedy wants your vote. On Iraq at least, he has bumbled to a place where giving it to him probably sends out a fairly clear signal. But as I plodded away from his office, I didn't feel sure that he and his colleagues really deserved it.

In November 2003, George W. Bush came to London, and a couple of hundred thousand people assembled to demonstrate their lack of hospitable spirit. Marvelling once again at the fact that a Labour government had caused me to take to the streets just as often as its dreaded predecessors, I was among them, pacing from the University of London to Trafalgar Square, where I was shouted at by such bespoke orators as Mick Rix, the then-leader of the train drivers' union ('Blair must go! Blair must go!' he chanted, rather desperately), and informed by my girlfriend that I had missed the fabled toppling of the papier-mâché statue of the President.

Half an hour or so before, I had found myself standing next to Lembit Öpik, the Liberal Democrat MP for the rural Welsh constituency of Montgomeryshire. Dressed in a Barbour jacket, accompanied by his assistant, and occasionally glancing at his pager, he had the slightly giddy air of a teenage truant. Though he seemed not to remember it, we'd met once before while contributing to a programme on BBC 5 Live – which I reminded him of, before rather earnestly letting rip with my misgivings about Charles Kennedy's woefully hesitant war rhetoric. He nodded a few times, and told me he'd pass my feelings on. I didn't believe for a moment that he would, but it was nice of him to pretend.

Lembit – his air of informal bonhomie rules out calling him Mr Öpik – speaks for the Lib Dems on both youth affairs and Northern Ireland (and was recently tipped by a *Times* article to become his party's first Prime Minister in 2023). He is the 37-year-old son of Estonian parents who brought him up in Belfast. Anagrams of his name – as the *Guardian*'s Simon Hoggart once pointed out – include 'I like to b MP' and 'I kil to be PM'. In the same article, centred around Lembit's campaign to be president of the Liberal Democrats, a party official called Tessa Munt told

Hoggart that Lembit was very skilled at 'touching the member-ship. He goes round the country touching people.'

You can see her point: give or take a slightly ill-advised fond-ness for asking parliamentary questions about asteroids, he oozes a contagious enthusiasm for both his party and the small victories that can occasionally be wrung from organised politics. There is also the frisson of middlebrow glamour provided by his engagement to the ITV weather forecaster and sometime *I'm a Celebrity* participant Siân Lloyd – though when we met again one summer Friday in his constituency, their relationship only intruded the once. Just before we parted company, his mobile phone trilled, and he briefly broke off to ask the caller to ring him back. 'That was Siân,' he said, trying to feign nonchalance but looking ever-so-slightly thrilled. 'She was just phoning for a gas.'

We talked in his office in Newtown, the pocket-sized market town that stands as his constituency's administrative centre. He served me tea in a gaudy George W. Bush mug ('Ironic,' he assured me), while he tugged on a cup of vegetable Slim-A-Soup and cast his mind back to our brief encounter at the march. Despite my scepticism, he claimed to have relayed what I'd said that day to Mr Kennedy. 'The point you made would have res-onated with most of the people who were there,' he assured me. 'And I wanted him to know that, because it's part of my job to lobby for a stronger message in those places where the party should be strong.

'The one time I was frustrated with the party was after the vote on the war had taken place in the Commons,' he continued. 'We let it sound like, "Oh well, the game's up – we're going to war now." I think we should have said, "We accept that we did not win this vote, but let this chamber and the country be clear: the Liberal Democrats were opposed to the war, and we're *still* opposed to the war: let's get our boys back with the minimum of killing of our people, and the minimum on the other side." Not doing that was a tactical mistake.'

My two hours of conversation with him hardly began promisingly. When he was fleshing out what drew him to the Liberal Democrats, my mind quietly boggled. 'I spent a couple of hours with Paddy Ashdown in 1989,' he said, slightly wistfully, 'and I thought, "I really believe in this guy."' His definition of his own politics was as fuzzy as those offered by his colleagues: 'What I'm doing in this party is trying to create a government which helps you be the best you can be without harming others.' And yet, despite all that, and his stereotypically Lib Dem rejection of the kind of first-principle thinking they dismiss as 'dogmatic' and 'ideological', he managed to convince me that he was just about on my side.

When we talked about the creeping privatisation of healthcare, he said that no one had yet explained to him how the necessity of profit could be squared with the NHS's imperative to allocate the optimum share of its resources to patient care. On tax, he enthusiastically talked up his party's commitment to a 50 per cent top rate: 'Lib Dem policy is to charge people who are very rich more tax. We want to use the best system yet devised for the redistribution of wealth, which is general taxation.' And when I raised the tangled messages I'd got from his colleagues on those kind of issues, he slightly angrily invited me to look at the Liberal Democrats' voting record. 'It's *absolutely* clear what we think,' he insisted, 'because in Parliament, when the rubber hit the road, we voted against Foundation Hospitals en masse. We voted on student tuition and top-up fees en masse. We were opposed to a whole pile of stuff on the railways en masse, and we were against the war en masse.'

What impressed me most of all was an honesty that made him by far the most consistent Liberal Democrat I met: an MP with a rare openness to the notion of following one's ideas to their logical conclusion, crystallised by his answer to a question about the Lib Dems' slightly schizoid pronouncements about tactical voting. It puzzled me, I said, that though his party was well known for building its campaigns around that notion, when presented with seats where they trailed a distant third and Labour were in with a shout of deposing a Tory, their spokes-people couldn't bring themselves to do the decent thing. If we were agreed that a Tory government was a much worse eventu-ality than the return of Mr Blair, then what would Lembit tell the voters of Boston and Skegness, where the 2001 election found the Conservatives at 19,750, Labour a mere 648 votes behind them, and the Lib Dems trailing at 7,721?

'I don't think this country should forgive the Conservatives for the way they ran it for eighteen years, for at least the same length of time,' he said. 'They did *so* much damage. And while I like to see the Liberal Democrat vote go up, I can still see the benefits of a tactical vote. In a sense, it's a rough and ready form of propor-tional representation: you're skipping your first preference and going straight to second. I think that, given the political realities of the world, we'd better fit in some tactical voting.'

Unfortunately, if Lembit Öpik made me feel newly relaxed about the prospect of prising myself away from the Labour Party and voting Liberal Democrat, there was one glaring snag: what with the Lib Dems' right-wingers in the ascendant and Charles

Kennedy fudging his way towards the next election, I wondered where he fitted in. When it came to their next set of election pledges and the pull his party might exert on some imagined minority Labour government, for example, would his kind of views actually count for much?

'My feeling,' he said, 'is that in the party high command, there's a significant group of people who would like to introduce what you might call free-market liberalism – the sort of thing that Thatcher was loosely associated with, and that goes down very well in the kind of Eastern European countries that have just joined the EU: a low tax burden, high degree of freedom and so on. I also think that, slightly ironically, some of those people would be willing to restrict the freedoms of, for example, workers in emergency services to strike, because they think that's an acceptable restriction to facilitate the greater good. But I think that as that seeps out into the wider party, it will be resisted.'

And what was the upshot of that kind of clash for the Liberal Democrats' next manifesto? Despite the rise of the party's free-marketeers, was it conceivable that it might contain, say, a pledge to undertake a comprehensive review of PFI?

'It *could* say something like that,' he said.

But did he think it *would*?

'An early draft might, but I think it would be heavily resisted by people like –' He stopped himself. 'Well, hang on – this is when you get into sophistry and semantics. You're talking about a negotiation within the party. You find a form of words which means two things, so both sides of the party can say, "We got what we wanted." And when we're in government, we'll sort it out then.'

At that point, I slightly raised my voice. That was absurdly frustrating, I said. On an issue like that, with the Tories and Labour seemingly united by a consensus that took no account of widespread public disquiet, the Lib Dems were surely missing an open political goal. They were certainly compromising their appeal to people like me.

'What I'm saying,' he began, 'is that the manifesto might be couched in softer terms than someone like me would like, and there are many people like me in the party. But if you step back from the manifesto, the difference between us and the Labour–Tory alternative is absolutely obvious. You may not get everything that you want, but you might get the same mood music that caused me to join the party in 1989. I couldn't have listed their policy agenda, but I knew how they made me *feel*.'

And so we arrived at my key difficulty. By and large, the Liberal Democrats made me feel uncomfortably muddled – a problem that was about to get much, much worse.

One afternoon in the spring of 2004, I met Mark Oaten, the Liberal Democrat MP for Winchester since 1997, and the party's home affairs spokesman. I had arranged to talk to him on the advice of a Liberal Democrat press officer who brimmed with admiration for his forward-thinking brilliance. She was not alone: a couple of months later, he appeared in a huge article in the *Observer* which listed eighty 'prodigiously talented young people who will shape our lives in the early twenty-first century'. He was placed alongside names as diverse as the singer from Franz Ferdinand, the historian Tristram Hunt and the editor of *Glamour* magazine, and accorded a blurb evidently written by someone with a flimsy grasp of the parliamentary hierarchy: 'One of the rising stars of the Liberal Democrats. His appointment as Shadow Home Secretary last October signalled a career that is on the up.'

If all that suggested a swashbuckling young radical, that didn't turn out to be quite the case. One of those fortysomething men who has both a baby-ish face and a thinning hairline, Mr Oaten was more Charlie Brown than Che Guevara. More importantly, as one of the founders of the Peel Group, an organisation set up to enhance the party's appeal to wavering Tories, he is widely seen as one of the key figures in the party's tumble to the right, fond of statements like this: 'Do we want to put the consumers at the heart of the debate? Do we want to come up with a form of delivery which means we have the best hospitals and schools for our constituents? Or are we going to just say, "No, it must always be the public services which do this"?'

Sitting in a parliamentary café, we began talking about his membership of the nascent SDP as a first-time voter repulsed by Thatcherism, but almost as alienated by the Labour Party: 'this shambolic outfit that was committed to withdrawing from Europe and a unilateral policy on nuclear arms, that looked tired and worn out, that looked scruffy, and that didn't appeal to an eighteen-year-old who wanted something that looked a little bit modern and different. And then,' he continued, his conversational tone suddenly brightening, 'this new modern party comes along that has its own credit cards, that has rather nice logos, that has a modern, professional media launch.'

He now sounded positively evangelical. 'They're wearing suits. They're driving round in Volvos. It's claret and chips. It was different, exciting, dynamic. There wasn't necessarily a philosophical belief: the important thing was, it wasn't Tory or Labour. And it was modern, it was different.'

The next bit was so startling that I had trouble maintaining my composure. 'I only really got a philosophical belief about three years ago,' he admitted. 'I've gone through this whole process as a pragmatic individual, who's just by quirk ended up in Parliament. It was only about three years ago that I got it. I suddenly was able to call myself a Liberal, which I'd found difficult to do in the past. It suddenly clicked. Before that, I'd become a Liberal Democrat, I'd got elected to Parliament – but I hadn't really defined what being a Liberal Democrat meant.'

But you must have known the kind of society you wanted to live in, I said. You surely had some idea of what the responsibilities of government should be. That's, you know, what politics is *based* on.

'But I'd taken that very much on a case-by-case basis, in a very pragmatic way,' he said. 'You know: what do I believe about immigration? What do I believe about Europe? What do I believe about the health service? I'd never really had a set of philosophical values. Once I got over this barrier of the word Liberal, I suddenly clicked that if you have a philosophical belief that being Liberal is being laissez-faire and not wanting a nanny state, you can suddenly start to impose that on a whole load of political situations. I've now been able to get my head around doing it.'

His belated enthusiasm for the idea of having a philosophy could be heard in a speech he'd given at the Liberal Democrats' 2004 spring conference which had mooted the idea of 'Tough Liberalism'. If the term superficially suggested the unlikely idea of individual freedom being miraculously squared with a populist emphasis on law and order, Oaten's speech fleshed out something slightly different: in his estimation, toughness was all about breaking with the repressive consensus that united the government, the Tories and the tabloid press. Rousing his audience into a burst of dislike for David Blunkett, he took issue with the Home Secretary's boast that news of Harold Shipman's suicide had made him want to open a bottle of champagne, his alleged role in introducing new Home Office powers to delay the release of the infamous Maxine Carr, and his endlessly knuckle-headed pronouncements on asylum. 'Being a Liberal Democrat home affairs spokesman means defending unpopular arguments,' he said. Cynics, of course, could allege that it was yet another example of the luxury of not having to worry about life as realistic contenders for government, but what the hell: hearing someone finally take issue with the Home Secretary's knee-jerk posturing was quite a thrill.

The day I spoke to him, however, I was keener to make sense of his beliefs about the future of the public services. Whereas his rhetoric on civil liberties marked out a clear divide between the Lib Dems and the government, when Mark Oaten spoke about health in particular, their differences became alarmingly blurred. Trawling through cuttings on the subject, I found proposals to contract out healthcare to charities and voluntary organisations, and statements of admiration for countries whose hospitals saw 'the private sector being used with some accountability'. One BBC profile ran as follows: 'Mr Oaten says he would like to see a system where patients can choose where to have their treatment, including in a "community hospital" which is funded by grants, trusts and private money.' These were not mere points of debate, either: given Oaten's position at the core of his party, at least some of them were apparently destined to make it into their next manifesto.

He courteously bought me a mug of tea, and attempted to explain the differences on public services that might divide the Liberal Democrats from the two main parties at the next election. Not much of what he had to say made sense, but I could scent a familiar enough agenda: objection to the allegedly tired old concept of state provision, and a vision of a new world in which the private sector would be zealously embraced.

'On public services and delivery, I think you'll find our health and education spokesmen much more open to putting the consumer at the heart of the choice,' he said, 'and getting less tangled up in the ideological argument between public and private. Where we'll be different from Labour is this . . .'

By way of illustrating the point he was about to make, he reached for three white plastic drink-stirrers and placed them in a row. Some tea had been spilled on the table, so two of them – which, I think, were meant to represent the Liberal Democrats and Labour – began to slide around uneasily.

· 'I suspect, although they are changing, where Labour will come to is where we are as well.' He picked the Labour stirrer out of its tea-puddle, and placed it a little nearer the Liberal Democrat one. 'But they'll still want to control very much from the centre. They cannot get themselves off the target culture.'

The thing was, I interjected, it was looking like the Labour Party were going to pre-empt accusations like that. 'Localism' – whatever that is – was apparently going to be a big part of the next Labour manifesto.

'Well, that's a shift. *That's a shift,*' he replied, underlining that it wasn't actually that much of a shift by leaving the Labour tea-stirrer exactly where it was. 'But that's where I think they were: consumer first but target-driven, and control-driven, and rewarding the good and penalising the bad. Their instincts are to centralise. Now . . .'

He reached for the third stirrer, lying slightly to the right of the tea-puddle, and then put it down again. 'Where I suspect the Tories have been heading is again, consumer choice, but actually looking at forms of private insurance, so actually it will not be free at the point of delivery, so there'll be some element of vouchers and things like that.'

He proudly pointed at the stirrer in the middle. 'And where I think *we* should be heading, where we actually *have* been heading, is new localism. *Genuinely* new localism, because we do it rather well, and we can let go, and we can experiment, and we want to have this genuine choice, and it's free at the point of delivery, but it's not target-driven, and there'll be experimentation, and there'll be different ways of doing things, and it won't just be public or private, but it'll also have an element of the mutual form of delivery, and experimentation with different kinds of services. *That*'s the difference.'

Alerted to the wonderfully clear, transparently epochal choices that face voters at the next election, I politely nodded, as one of the tea-stirrers slowly floated off the table.

2 Hospitals

'If this is what Blair has in mind for the NHS, watch out.'

On Friday, 16 June 2000, Tony Blair arrived in Carlisle. He was there to open the new Cumberland Infirmary, built at a cost of £87 million and hailed as 'the first public hospital to be built with private money'. He breezed into the hospital's gleaming, light-soaked atrium, surrounded by a gaggle of senior managers, photographers and reporters, and eventually gave a brief speech. 'I congratulate everyone involved in the design and construction of this magnificent new hospital,' he said, 'which is an excellent example of public–private partnership in practice. It symbolises much of what we have been trying to do for the health service.'

The Cumberland Infirmary was built as part of the Private Finance Initiative, a policy (also known as Public Private Partnership) that New Labour had inherited from the Conservatives and decisively extended into the NHS. PFI's history contained plenty to worry about – the first ever PFI project, a privately-run causeway on the Isle of Skye, had led to something not far short of a local mutiny – but the government obviously thought the benefits outweighed the drawbacks. On a cynical level, you could see their point: aside from PFI's other alleged benefits to the NHS, it meant that new hospitals could be rolled out without the government having to fret too much about the effects on the public purse. The private sector would come up with the funds, see to everything apart from the medical side of things – and, for better or worse, expect to turn a healthy profit.

The Cumberland Infirmary was built, owned and partly run by a private consortium headed by the construction firm Amec. When they first released news of their involvement in PFI's extension into the health service, their share price skyrocketed. And small wonder: their deal at the Cumberland Infirmary meant they and their partners would own the hospital for at least thirty years, being paid an annual sum (rent, in all but name) by the local NHS Trust that would start out at £11 million and rise with inflation. Here, it seemed, was capitalism without any of its irritatingly risky aspects: simply a fantastically lucrative contract that stretched into the future. Amec were not alone in their luck: Interserve, one of their consortium partners, had been handed the contract to deliver all the new hospital's 'non-clinical support services' – cleaning, catering, security, patient telephones – until 2045. In case anyone wondered what would happen if anything went wrong, there was an option to review after thirty years.

The recent history of the Cumberland Infirmary was scattered with other figures that would surely cause any Labour Party supporter at least passing alarm. As part of Interserve's contract, 326 people had been transferred from the public to private sector, many of them finding that shift patterns and working practices had suddenly been altered with a view to cutting costs. Yet more worryingly, compared to the two Carlisle hospitals that the Infirmary had been built to replace, the number of beds had fallen by ninety.

Some of the Infirmary's other problems couldn't be quite as tightly quantified, but were no less worrying. A year after Mr Blair's visit, operating theatres were plunged into darkness by a twenty-minute power cut, caused by the failure of the hospital's emergency generators. Faulty plumbing meant that, on two occasions, cardiac patients and women in the maternity wards had been soaked by water and effluent. For some reason, no one had thought to build a dedicated storage space for X-rays and copies of patient records: for the time being, they were stored in an old annexe, which involved a fifteen-minute round trip for any nurse or doctor.

The source of all these woes wasn't too hard to identify: the hospital's problems were rooted in the cost-watching and corner-cutting that came with the necessity of making shareholders a dividend. 'The developers always think of the bottom line,' one Cumberland Infirmary doctor told the BBC in 2001. 'You have to hold a gun to their head to get them to repair anything. If this is what Blair has in mind for the NHS, watch out.'

For reasons of curiosity rather than ill health, I paid a visit to the Infirmary in July last year. I arrived on a sunny Tuesday morning, and drove into the hospital's pay-and-display car park. The ticket machine, unfortunately, was broken. 'Don't worry about it,' said a passing attendant. 'Just leave your car. It'll be fine. It's been like that for a while.' As I soon discovered, the Cumberland Infirmary was that kind of place.

I had fifteen minutes before my first appointment, so I thought I'd have a brief look around. I particularly wanted to see the atrium, described by some observers as an 'airy internal mall'. 'Psychologically, it's like being outside,' one of the Consortium's architectural consultants had enthused. 'It's like walking down a high street, where you bump into people you know.' It certainly looked nice, but its history had been problem-ridden. Soon after the Infirmary had opened its doors, it became clear that a lack of air conditioning meant that temperatures could get as high as 110° Fahrenheit. The day I visited, a new glitch was in evidence: some of the glass panes that ringed each of the atrium's three levels had mysteriously exploded, showering people below in broken glass. For the time being, the panes were draped with an ugly green tarpaulin.

Twenty minutes later, I was sitting in the office of Linda Weightman, the full-time convenor at the Infirmary for Unison, the public sector union. With a mixture of anger, upset and bafflement, she talked me through the story of the last four years. 'I'm sick to death of saying it,' she said at one point. 'PFI is a nightmare.'

When the Cumberland Infirmary opened, Linda was a scrubs nurse: one of those people who jump to attention when the surgeon says 'Scalpel' or 'Swab'. In the course of her work, she had witnessed all manner of mishaps – like 2001's power cut. 'The electricity just *failed*,' she said. 'And the emergency generator didn't work, but they didn't know that it didn't work because they'd never tested it. There were people in theatres who were being operated on – but there's a battery life within the equipment that they use and the lighting, so they were alright. But the recovery room went blacker than night. My friend was working in recovery and the patients were very, very frightened. There were people going round with torches saying, "Are you alright?" Patients were stuck in scanners in the X-ray department. They were manually bagging people in ITU.'

ITU, I knew, stood for Intensive Therapy Unit: the place where patients were kept on life-support machines. But what did 'manually bagging people' involve?

'You have a big bag, like a bellows. That's what enables people to breathe. And the nurses were working those, by hand, for twenty minutes – which I can tell you is jolly hard work.'

One of her most horrifying memories related to an operation she had taken part in using the new hospital's day-unit theatres. Some of the consultants employed by the Infirmary had expressed concern about the facilities that had been provided; it had taken, Linda said, an awful lot of persuasion to convince them to come and work there. One orthopaedic consultant in particular expressed such scepticism that the prospect of him working in the day unit seemed pretty slim, but he eventually agreed to give it a try.

'The first operation that we were doing was an arthroscopy, on a knee – you put a camera into the knee,' said Linda. 'Now, this consultant is very, very picky about sterility and everything: it all has to be done to the letter. So, I was there with my trolley, the patient was behind me, awake, just about to be anaesthetised – and the bloody window blew open. Just, *boom*!

'You can't have windows that open in theatres. But they hadn't put sealed window units in. They *should* have done, but what they put in were windows that you could open – and put them in a locked position, squirted glue in, and then taken the handles off. That was supposed to be a sealed unit – as opposed to a proper sealed unit that won't open at all.

'The consultant said, "What the hell is going on?" All this wind and dust was blowing in. He took his gloves off, stamped his feet, and said "That's it! I'm never coming back again!" Anyway, the lads from the consortium came, and one of them said to me, "They didn't put sealed windows in anywhere. These are just bog-standard double-glazed windows."'

The anger focused on such failures was heightened by the fact that, PFI being what it was, the Infirmary's private consortium was making a profit: 45 per cent of their £11 million a year rent, according to one of Linda Weightman's sources in the hospital's senior management. One hesitates to make a point so glib, but that kind of money could have surely paid for very nice windows indeed.

The Private Finance Initiative's malign aspects are not just down to its in-built emphasis on corner-cutting in the service of profit. Even if the consortia decided to turn their usual codes of practice on their head and relegate the profit motive to a lowly priority, PFI would still represent something not far short of a scandal. The reason is twofold: it lies in both the difference between the terms on which money is lent to the government or private companies, and the fact that PFI amounts to a very expensive kind of mortgage.

When the government borrows money, it is charged rates of interest that reflect the certainty of the funds being repaid – the state, after all, is highly unlikely to go bankrupt. Private firms, by contrast, must pay the kind of rates that reflect a greater degree of risk. Thus, the rent paid to them under PFI includes a hefty share that, were the project kept within the public sector, could go on patient care. On top of that, there is the fact that, over the length of the contract, the cash handed to the consortia far exceeds the actual cost of the project. You get your school or hospital quickly enough, but decades down the line public money is still paying for it. The Cumberland Infirmary cost £87 million; over time, the taxpayer will pay well over £400 million. More alarmingly still, on Linda Weightman's figures, £180 million of that will be clear profit for the consortium. You could build two more Cumberland Infirmaries with that sum of money, with cash to spare.

Also, there is a seemingly iron rule whereby the figures agreed when consortia are awarded their contracts are far outstripped by the initial building and running costs. At that point, the local Health Trust has little option but to renegotiate, come up with the extra money, and cut services elsewhere. A PFI hospital in Dartford, for example, saw a rise of 41 per cent, and consequent cuts in services to people with learning difficulties and the local provision of district nurses. In Worcester, a mind-boggling hike of 127 per cent led to the winding-down of another hospital in nearby Kidderminster; the result was an old-fashioned public revolt and the defeat of the local Labour MP at the 2001 election (more of which later).

Aside from all that, there is the role in PFI of service companies – the firms who make their money by swallowing up the NHS's so-called ancillary facilities. At the Cumberland Infirmary, these were seen to by the Interserve Group, whose unctuous on-site slogan is 'Partnering our business with your needs'. Interserve have an annual turnover of £1.2 billion and employ 13,000 people around the world. The provision of hospital services is merely one of their areas of expertise: their recent commissions have included work on a railway in Taiwan, a bridge in Hong Kong, a new grandstand at Lord's and a handful of freshly-proposed schools in Telford.

The day I was in Carlisle, I met another Linda: Linda Devlin. Up until the end of 1999, she was employed as an NHS cook. She used to wear a traditional white catering uniform with an apron, and prepare the food that was served to patients from scratch. If, for example, you ordered a roast dinner, it came to Linda and her colleagues in the form of raw vegetables and meat, and was turned into a hot meal in a hospital kitchen. Moreover, the hospital in which she worked operated a menu system whereby patients ordered their three daily meals twenty-four hours in advance, to ensure that everyone got what they wanted and to reduce waste.

All that had come to an end with the advent of PFI. These days, Linda wore a blue sweatshirt printed with Interserve's logo – a kind of wonky palm tree-type thing, perhaps meant to look like a human figure with five arms – and her culinary responsibilities involved nothing more complicated than receiving deliveries of ready-cooked meals from a storage depot in Manchester, extracting them from their packaging and loading them into a trolley that also served to heat the food up or keep it cold. Worse still, the menu system was now a distant memory: instead, Interserve employees second-guessed what patients and staff might choose and placed their twice-weekly orders accordingly. The food that was left over – and there was a lot, apparently – was simply thrown away.

'The new trolley system is very bad,' Linda told me. 'It'll heat things that are meant to be cold, and keep things cold that are meant to be hot, or burn things. You get a lot of congealed food on plates. Say it was macaroni cheese – when it's cooked too much, it just congeals, and goes brown, and then the patients look at it and say, "Well, I don't want that."'

Her new employers, it seemed, based all their decisions on a simple enough formula: the minimisation of cost. 'They're always trying to cut down,' she said. 'They're only allowed to spend so many hundred pounds a month on, say, replacing cutlery and crockery – so you're not allowed to have it when you need it. There's always a big debate about whether you can really have it, or whether they can afford it. They'd sooner try and pinch it from somewhere else before they'd let you buy some more.'

Anyone conversant with the most basic laws of corporate culture could have foreseen what all this would lead to: with management placing such a stifling emphasis on keeping overheads down – obvious notice of which had been served by the arrival of Linda Devlin's hated 'cook-chill' method – staff morale had tumbled. The problem, in her telling of the story, was only made worse by Interserve's candour about their dried-up priorities. Private enterprise, driven by competition, usually claims that it attaches overwhelming importance to the idea of customer service. Given Interserve's forty-five-year contract, however, none of that seemed to count for very much – as some of their senior employees had apparently admitted.

'Before, everybody was fairly glad to come to work,' Linda told me. 'They enjoyed being at work, because everybody got on well, and you did your job, and the boss was pleased. But now, *nobody cares*. Even the manager couldn't care. He said to me once, about the hospital dining room, "I couldn't care less if nobody came in here to eat." What sort of attitude is that? You should be encouraging people to come in.'

There was one question I particularly wanted to ask Linda Devlin. I probably sounded wildly naive, but anyway: You used to work for the Health Service, I said. And that usually implies one thing in particular: some idea of public service – of, you know, helping the sick and infirm.

'Yes,' she replied. 'That's true.' She sounded simultaneously nostalgic and quietly furious.

And is there any part of you that still feels that you're doing that?

'No. I don't. Because . . . Well, the firm don't care who does what, or how they do it – they just want to tick boxes. And the other thing that really gets you is a feeling that now, with the rest of the people who work here, it's very Them and Us. We're the bad ones: the Interserve workers. The people who work for the Trust are the good guys. There's never been the same relationship as there was before, with nursing staff, or office staff, or anybody.'

If Linda felt suddenly isolated from other hospital staff, she was not alone. As Linda Weightman told me, one of the saddest effects of PFI at the Cumberland Infirmary had been a sudden, yawning division between the people who were employed by the NHS, and those unlucky enough to be contracted to Interserve. It was exacerbated by the fact that the Infirmary's ancillary staff now operated in the world of scythed-down costs and job cuts – worrying enough when it came to the catering, but taken into the realms of abject horror by what had happened with the hospital's cleaning. She showed me a recent check-list prepared by the North Cumbria NHS Trust's Cleaning Audit Team. Two items in particular leapt out: 'Clock in atrium is covered in dust, spiders' webs and dead flies. As are the vents'; 'Areas around entrances are littered with cigarette ends, crisp packets and cups. This is unsightly and smells, and gives the hospital a bad image.'

'When everybody worked for the hospital,' she explained, 'the domestics – or the pink ladies as we called them then – had *pride*. The skirting boards were clean, the table tops were absolutely pristine. And that was because they were on the same side. Hospitals are not just made up of doctors and nurses; they're made of admin and clerical people, secretaries, porters, the people who work as cleaners and ancillary staff. And they were included in the hospital team. If you went out at Christmas for a Christmas meal, you took the cleaner with you, because she'd worked on your ward for a long time. She could have been here twenty-five years. Twenty-five years earning appalling wages – but because there was this camaraderie, and everybody pulled together, it didn't seem to matter. There was team spirit.

'And what they did, when those people were sold out because of the plans for PFI – that was decimated. The unions told the management, time and time again, Did they not realise what they were doing to their workforce? They just didn't seem to take on the psychological implications, the fact that there would be two separate entities: the people who worked for the Trust, and the people who work for the private company.'

Cleaners, porters and caterers are a large but often unacknowledged part of the NHS. When people talk about New Labour's privatisation schemes eroding the public sector ethos, it's perhaps tempting to think that such talk couldn't possibly apply to them or their relationship with doctors and nurses. In the case of Charles Kennedy, such thinking means he can square his occasional hand-wringing about changing the 'dynamic' of public sector employees with his belief that pushing ancillary staff towards the private sector is 'not necessarily beyond the pale'. My visit to the Cumberland Infirmary proved one thing beyond doubt: it surely should be.

In addition, the time I spent in Carlisle left me with the abiding memory of Linda Weightman's righteous ire about what had happened to her hospital. She expressed it in the kind of terms that Mr Blair and his allies would doubtless see as archaic and outmoded – hopelessly *ideological*, to use a very modern pejorative – but the incongruity of her words only served to increase their force. New Labour might claim to found its policies in the notion of 'what works'; Linda by contrast, was one of those all-but-disenfranchised people who craved for a politics founded on first principles. 'You should never make money out of sick people,' she said. 'You ask the staff in this hospital and they'll tell you: it's *immoral* to make money out of people who are ill.'

The underlying problems that have blighted the Cumberland Infirmary have reared up in just about all PFI hospital projects. Most significantly, in such places as Dartford and Bishop Auckland and Halifax and Hereford, bed numbers in PFI hospitals relative to those they replaced have been cut by an average of around 30 per cent. Though the government is wont to talk about the expansion of the NHS since it arrived in power, PFI's bed-cutting has made a contribution to a particularly striking statistic: according to the Department of Health's own figures, since 1997 the actual number of hospital beds has fallen by 15,000.

PFI is also emblematic of a new kind of NHS, in which every penny is wrung from hospitals' infrastructure and profit very often seems to be king. An instructive example lies in the provision of patient telephones. In eighty-four hospitals, with another fifty to follow, the requisite contract has been handed to Patientline, who charge sky-high rates to those phoning their hospitalised friends and family. 'Patientline is focused on providing services for patients and remains committed to improving the hospital experience,' says its website; should you wish to check on one of your kith and kin at a Patientline hospital, you will be charged 39p cheap rate and 49p at peak times.

As mentioned above, in one British town, PFI led to a genuine popular rebellion. From 1999 onwards, skyrocketing costs at the new Worcester Royal PFI hospital led to the shrinking of services at the main hospital eighteen miles away in Kidderminster – most notably, the Accident and Emergency Department was downgraded to a Minor Injuries Unit. The consequences were occasionally tragic: in February 2001, for example, a pensioner who lived five minutes from the Kidderminster hospital died during the 50-minute journey to Worcester that PFI had made inescapable.

In the meantime, an ad hoc anti-PFI party called Health Concern had become the biggest single party in the local District Council; and at the 2001 election, one David Lock – who had beaten the sitting Tory in 1997 – was trounced by a Health Concern candidate, Dr Richard Taylor, a retired consultant who had put in twenty-three years of service at Kidderminster Hospital. The most striking passage in his victory speech ran as follows: 'I view this as a tremendous reaction from the people against a very powerful government, against a very powerful political system that overrides the will of the people.' In the words of the *Observer*, 'Worcester women and Mondeo men left their pebble-dashed houses to vote for the former consultant from Kidderminster Hospital because of the damage the wildly imprudent costs of allowing the private sector to run hospitals inflicted on Middle England.'

New Labour, however, has hardly been chastened. In July 2004, the Health Secretary John Reid announced plans for fifteen more NHS PFI projects, in such places as Taunton, Bristol,

Leeds and Liverpool. Meanwhile, PFI has gone international: the construction firms and service companies at the heart of PFI are only too happy to assist a very New Labour kind of export drive, assisting with projects in Canada, Australia, New Zealand, South Africa and the Far East.

More alarmingly still, in Britain, PFI is being rolled out into all areas of the public sector. There are now PFI police stations and prisons. In 2002, David Miliband told *The Times* that there would be 'no holds barred' in the extension of PFI to the UK's schools. 'PFI has transformed many schools,' he said, 'and this will help us transform standards.'

Unfortunately, though the likes of Mr Miliband seem happily unaware of it, the private sector is characterised not just by Mr Blair's beloved efficiency and dynamism. You don't get that aspect without a large degree of risk and uncertainty. And such is one of PFI's other key weaknesses, as proved by reports like this (from the *Scotsman*, 17 January 2004):

SCHOOL BOOKS RETURNED TO LIBRARY AFTER PPP FIASCO
School books impounded by a storage firm which hasn't been paid as a result of the East Lothian public-private partnership fiasco have finally been returned to pupils.

Computer equipment and books from Musselburgh Grammar's library had been unavailable since main PPP contractor Ballast UK went into administration about four months ago, bringing the £43 million refurbishment project to a halt.

But despite still being owed money, Pickfords has now agreed to release the items as a 'gesture of goodwill'. Headteacher Yvonne Mackie said: 'We are overjoyed that the library facilities have been returned to us, and the library is up and running again.'

She added: 'Running a school without a library has been very diffi-cult and the teachers and staff have really worked hard together to minimise the effect it had on our pupils.'

Teachers at Musselburgh Grammar and two other affected schools have already asked the Scottish Qualifications Authority for special dispensation as a result of the disruption.

Sub-contractors who claim they are still owed £5 million for work on the stalled scheme revealed earlier this week that they are set to hire corporate lawyers in a bid to recoup their losses. Balfour Beatty is currently in negotiations to take over the troubled project and work could get under way as soon as next month.

In his speech to the 2002 Labour Party Conference, Tony Blair attempted to take on the critics of PFI, making reference to the alleged views of his own constituents on the new wards and classrooms that were springing up all over Britain. 'They don't care who builds them, so long as they're built,' he said. '*I* don't care who builds them, so long as they're on cost, on budget, and helping to deliver a better NHS and better state schools for the people of Sedgefield and every other constituency in the land.'

Perhaps Mr Blair hadn't heard about the skyrocketing bills, renegotiated contracts, power cuts, leaking drains, demoralised staff and reductions in bed numbers. 'Come *on*,' he pleaded with his audience. 'This isn't the betrayal of public services. It's their renewal. All that is happening is that here, as round the rest of the world, we are dividing means and ends.'

New Labour, in other words, was privatising its way towards a public service utopia. His reasoning was delusional, but very modern: much the same kind of logic one sees in those magazines that claim that people can somehow eat themselves thin.

3 The Labour Party

'We're very loyal to our leaders.'

If the time I spent in Carlisle had only served to heighten my queasiness about voting Labour, the Lib Dems' mixed-up, alarmingly vague, frequently quasi-Blairite pronouncements hadn't offered all that much of an alternative. That said, even if Charles Kennedy *et al* had been brimming with incisive analysis and first-principle commitments, I would probably still have been left a few yards from complete conversion – for somewhere close to my soul, there still lurked an intuitive loyalty to the party I had joined back in the 1980s.

When I came to speak to Labour people, I therefore knew exactly what I was after: arguments that might somehow separate the Blairites from the party as a whole, and thereby assure me that you could somehow vote Labour in an anti-New Labour kind of way. I was sceptical about the chances of it sounding convincing, but still: there seemed to be no shortage of people who thought that kind of political doublethink was at least tenable. First of all, though, I wanted to track down a figure from my far-off days as a teenage activist – someone who was now at the very heart of what the government was up to.

Back in the mid-80s, my brief period as secretary of the Tatton Labour Party Young Socialists was mostly spent trying to fight a gang of Trotskyists – sellers of the newspaper called *Militant*, most weekends – who looked like The Housemartins but behaved like the mafia. In the back room of the White Bear, the shabby pub in Knutsford where we held our monthly meetings, Mrs Thatcher would usually recede into the distance while they accused me of 'not knowing my history', and I wondered how I had come from enthusiastically reading leaflets at Billy Bragg concerts to fighting off determined 'entryists' with an unhealthy interest in dead Russians.

On the occasions when I would surface from all the in-fighting and commune with the party's grown-ups, a recurrent presence was a woman named Hazel Blears, then a thirty-year-old solicitor who had been selected as Tatton's Prospective Labour Candidate. She had a grisly job, attempting to take on the Conservatives in a constituency that was among the safest Tory heartlands in the country. Her opponent, though at the time he was a barely known parliamentary journeyman, was Neil Hamilton, a man who would occasionally pace around Wilmslow, Knutsford and Northwich – accompanied by his wife, Christine – wearing the brazen smile of someone who believed himself to be invincible.

He was, back then – but Hazel, a doughty, diminutive woman in Ben Elton glasses, was determined to fight Tatton as if it was up for grabs. To that end, she would drive into deepest Cheshire from her home in central Manchester, and energise those of us who had volunteered to assist her. My clearest memory of her is at the first meeting of our Young Socialists branch, surveying a mixed gaggle of smirking Trots and adolescent political innocents, and telling us that no matter how out-there our politics were, the older elements of the party would do well to listen to us. 'I know that some people think the YS is too radical,' she said, putting down her half of bitter. 'But I think that that radicalism is a good thing. It keeps the party on its toes. It reminds them of what's important.'

In 1997, Hazel Blears was elected to Parliament as the MP for the safe Labour constituency of Salford. She was soon recruited as the Parliamentary Private Secretary to the devout Blairite Alan Milburn, following him from a brief spell as a health minister, through the Treasury, and back to health for his four-year spell at the top. By 2002, she was the Minister in charge of Public Health; the following year, she was recruited by David Blunkett to the Home Office. Mere days before we met, she was given the brief of Minister for Counter-Terrorism; should the Blairites' hegemony survive the next election, it may only be a matter of time before she makes into the Cabinet. Throughout all this, happily liberated from being kept on her toes, her parliamentary voting behaviour has been as impeccably New Labour as her jobs demanded: pro-war, tuition fees and Foundation Hospitals, but – lest anyone think socialism is somehow imperilled – fiercely anti when it comes to the annual bunfight about foxhunting.

On account of her new place at the head of the struggle against the world's *jihadists*, she has recently been pushed dizzyingly close to the front pages. In the words of a *Daily Telegraph* profile, 'With her perfectly painted lips and neatly pressed red suit, Miss Blears does not look like the leader of Britain's fight against terrorism. She is 4 feet 10½ inches tall, runs a weekly Commons tap-dancing group and is famous for riding a vintage Italian motorbike. She is the minister responsible for tracking down Osama Bin Laden and preventing an Al Qaeda attack.' The paper accompanied its story with a picture of a leather-clad Hazel astride her beloved motorcycle, with the headline 'The Minister with Perfect Lipstick on the Trail of Bin Laden'. It seemed to be implying that, like some New Labour version of Lara Croft, she was about to put on her helmet and race after him.

Thinking she might just remember me from the dark days of the 80s, I emailed Hazel and asked if she'd be interested in talking to me. We arranged to meet one Friday afternoon at her constituency office. As it turned out, she saw to her constituency business from a three-room annexe to a mock-Tudor former nursing home which now houses a huge collection of literature known as the Salford Working Class Movement Library. I snuck a quick look inside on the way to the loo: draped with banners for Socialist Sunday Schools, and stuffed with books by such far-flung left-wing titans as Marx and Engels and Antonio Gramsci, it gave off the musty-smelling scent of things now all but vanished: a Labour Party made up of horny-handed auto-didacts, long meetings about composite motions, the idea that the Great Leap Forward might be only a few hard years away. The fact that the Blears office sat next to all the relics seemed, in its own mundane way, to provide a wonderfully bathetic conclusion to the library's half-century history.

Seventeen years on, she was markedly thinner, and the glasses had gone. We managed a few minutes of small talk about Tatton and our different lives since, but Hazel and I didn't really get along. Contrary to her and her colleagues' professed fondness for an honest and open debate – a 'Big Conversation', even – she quickly seemed to scent my old-fashioned opinions, and didn't have much patience with them. There was precious little common ground; the experience reminded me of evenings at the White Bear in the company of the Tatton Trotskyists, though this time knowing my history was less of an issue. In Hazel

Blears' estimation, I had made the altogether more serious error of not surrendering to my future.

What I was up against, it transpired, was a warped, flatly surreal kind of class politics, uprooted from their centuries-long foundation in such old-fashioned notions as redistributive taxation, free education for all and the idea that no one should wring a profit out of the old and infirm, and transplanted into the topsy-turvy world created by New Labour. Hazel and her friends were busy building a gleaming idyll where PFI hospitals and schools went up at the rate of three a week, and ever-increasing millions gleefully went to university without worrying about the prospect of vast debt; only bourgeois, *Guardian*-reading stick-in-the-muds like me worried about where all of it was taking us. Such, it seemed, was the explanation for her strikingly un-Blairite habit of referring to the working class, and – perhaps – the fact that, at crucial parts of particular arguments, her Mancunian accent seemed to get a lot stronger.

We talked at first about what I politely called her political journey. 'Being a parliamentary candidate in 1987 in Tatton was a huge growing-up experience,' she explained, 'and I think I was a changed person when I came out of that. I understood that you couldn't just rail against everything – you had to have positive proposals to put forward. You had to turn from somebody who'd spent all of the Thatcher years passing resolutions, being appalled about things, into trying to have a bit more of a constructive policy platform – just recognising the reality of the world a bit more.'

Thus, her view of objections to building and running schools and hospitals under the PFI programme was that they were 'theoretical', and the simple fact that scores of new projects were underway more than justified it ('I don't regard PFI as fundamentally undermining my Labour Party values, 'cos I've just got a brand new High School'). Despite the large-scale absence of supporting proof, Hazel also held fast to the realpolitik whereby 'Tony Blair was genuinely acting as a cautionary influence on the Bush administration.'

Perhaps most strikingly of all, when the real world provided stacked-up evidence against her viewpoint, she seemed to have mastered the habit of shutting off. When I explained that my opposition to war in Iraq was partly based on political queasiness about the agenda of such America neo-conservatives as Donald Rumsfeld and Paul Wolfowitz, she simply said, 'I don't really take a view about that so much. It's not something that I'm hugely exercised about.' As the minister in charge of counter-terrorism, she probably should be; a lot of the people she's up against certainly are.

Raising the deeply Blairite concept of 'tough choices', I wondered whether, called to vote for the annihilation of free higher education, or the bombing of Iraq, or the creation of Foundation Hospitals, Hazel had had her own gristly moments.

'Erm . . . I don't think I've ever had to really swallow hard and sort of grit my teeth and think, "I'm going to accept this policy even though I really don't like it,"' she said. 'I genuinely haven't had moments like that. And that's probably because my own personal journey's mirrored the political journey of the party. I've struggled with some decisions – like Iraq. I think most of us struggled with Iraq, as to whether it was the right thing to do.' (Despite the reduction of the country to an anarchic wreck, it was, of course – because 'people recognised that the alternative has having a dictator in place.')

And then we hit a particularly illuminating chunk of conversation: five minutes in which I would sail deep into the contorted doublethink that often passes for the government's abiding philosophy. She was about to hold forth about the controversy surrounding variable top-up fees, and the argument that allowing the UK's most upscale universities to charge more than lowlier institutions would put off prospective students from some social backgrounds and thereby turn them into middle-class closed shops.

'I think that's the biggest con-trick in the world,' she said. 'If you look at my constituency, most of my young people will benefit enormously, from getting grants re-introduced, from getting fees remitted. I'm actually quite angry about it, because I think that the opponents of that measure in our party see Oxford and Cambridge as the pinnacle of achievement, and are just as deluded about all that academic ivory-tower stuff as anybody in the Tory party. It was portrayed as, "I had a chance to go to Oxford, and as a result of this proposal, nobody else will ever have a chance to do that." Try asking round my community how many people have a chance of going to Oxford. If those people thought about it properly, and were really rooted in communities like mine, they would see that the whole argument about tuition fees is a complete sham.'

Now, if Hazel Blears meant what I thought she meant, she was of the opinion that fretting about working-class students going to Oxford and Cambridge actually implied an elitist emphasis on those elitist institutions, which were probably best left alone to carry on being elitist. This was strange enough; what followed was yet stranger.

One of the things I didn't like in the government's pro-fees rhetoric, I said, was the underlying emphasis on education as an individual good: the idea that going to university vastly upped one's earning potential and therefore obliged all those lucky students to cough up. This was no-such-thing-as-society stuff, as far as I could make out, neglecting the idea that all kinds of graduates justify the cost of their education in terms of its benefit to the rest of us.

'I think it's a bit of both,' said Hazel. 'It's undoubtedly a social good, because we want people to be better educated, we want them to be more literate, we want them to be more thinking individuals. But it's also a personal good, in that when you ask people on pretty low wages to continually stump up through higher taxes, which would have been the alternative –'

Well, I countered, maybe it actually wouldn't. Perhaps if the Labour Party rediscovered a mere fraction of its old belief in equality and you lot introduced a slightly more progressive taxation system, that scenario would be neatly avoided.

'Well, it might, it might not. You know, for years and years and years, low-paid people have subsidised middle-class people going to university, and I don't think that's necessarily the way things should be.'

The idea is, I said, a lot of graduates enter occupations that benefit people at the lower end of the social scale: doctors, teachers, social workers – *politicians*, even.

'But when I saw that young woman on television saying, "I am going to be a doctor, and I want to do such good work for all these poor people", I had to turn the television off. It made me feel ill. I thought it was. patronising claptrap.'

This was a reference to Julia Prague, a fleetingly famous nineteen-year-old who appeared on a *Newsnight* special in January

2004, pitching into Mr Blair about the debt she would amass in her six years as a medical student, and taking issue with a New Labour argument – peddled two years before, by the then-higher education minister Margaret Hodge – about the alleged injustice of 'the dustman subsidising the doctor'.

As I later discovered, Julia's words were slightly different from Hazel's recollection. She actually said this: 'I'm from an average middle-class background. I went to the local comprehensive. I am the first in my family to go to university. I think it will be students from my sort of background who will be most deterred. They will know that they won't get the financial help such as you are suggesting for the poorer student, [and] they don't have vast amounts of inherited wealth to call upon. They will be especially deterred from doing the long courses such as medicine. We have got a huge shortage of doctors and it will be the middle-class students who will be most pushed away.' On the dustman argument, meanwhile, she made the not-unreasonable point that 'when he has the heart attack he will be pleased that I went to university and graduated as a doctor. Therefore he should contribute towards the cost.'

Even if I took Hazel at her word and accepted that poor young Julia was a paternalist bourgeois with a condescending wish to help those less fortunate than herself, I thought the ferocity of her response to the idea was a bit misplaced. What if Julia, like some latter-day Florence Nightingale, thought that was her vocation? It has its upsides, after all.

'Yeah, well, maybe. But what about the binman who empties her bins? She couldn't live without somebody being prepared to empty her bins. And what do they get paid? She's going to be on sixty, seventy, eighty grand a year.'

And there's a reason for that, I said. Doctors have to be paid that much to attract people of the right quality into the profession.

In retrospect, I cannot quite believe what she said next. But it's there on the tape, unmistakably. 'And we don't have to pay people to empty bins to that extent?'

Well, no, we don't, I said. It's bound up with a concept known as transfer earnings, explained in most basic economics textbooks. You can find more people who are capable of being binmen. And, come to think of it, their lowlier salaries probably reflect the fact that it doesn't cost quite as much to train them.

'Well, it depends,' said Hazel Blears, preparing to cut through the last lengths of rope that tethered her argument to the demands of good sense, and serving notice of her departure by sounding a bit like John Prescott. 'It depends if it's the job market about doctors [sic], or is it a kind of restrictive profession, or, you know, what are the factors as to why it's so limited and people are not out there queuing up and, you know, the numbers are controlled by the GMC, and goodness knows what. There's an awful lot of other issues behind that.'

Twenty minutes later, I was disconsolately walking back towards the middle of Manchester, having succumbed to a feeling of bleak dejection.

On a number of the occasions when I went to meet MPs, I whiled away a lot of time in the foyer of Portcullis House, the vast building that partly addressed the Houses of Parliament's chronic lack of office space, but did so at the kind of cost that – as with the Scottish Parliament building – is frequently held up as a symbol of the chasm that lies between party politics and the

ordinary world. Built to 'last 200 years', with a ventilation system that 'filters fresh air through the carpets', its cost worked
out at around £235 million, which given the 210 MPs who were
allowed in, worked out at over £1 million per head. To the delight
of the broadcast and print media, this included £150,000 spent
on the hire of twelve fig trees, which – as it turned out – only
secured them for five years. 'To cost that amount of money,' said
a man from *Gardener's Question Time*, 'the species would have
to be so rare that I wouldn't even know about it.' He went on:
'They're the most boring tree imaginable, they don't really
flower, and the fruit isn't even edible.'

One of the distinguishing features of Portcullis House, aside
from policemen who somehow manage to hold light-hearted
conversations with the receptionists while keeping their fingers
on the triggers of machine guns, is the seemingly endless traffic of
ambitious young men, there to meet this or that MP, and thereby
advance their political careers. Here, the fact that the archetypal
MP now leaves university, shuffles to Westminster and experi-
ences alarmingly little of life among the rest of us is made flesh:
aspirant Blairites (Joe 90 glasses, slightly garish ties, suits with the
faintest hint of designer flash) queue for the security X-ray
machine next to ascendant Conservatives (striped shirts,
paunches, brogues, the usual), united by that strange effect
whereby would-be politicos manage to occupy a non-specific
age bracket somewhere between twenty-four and thirty-eight.

One day in early spring – the day the Spanish socialists won
the country's elections, for what it's worth – I stood in line
behind a towering young man whose attire all but confirmed
what he was doing there. And so it proved: 'I'm here to see David
Willetts,' he told the woman behind the reception desk, with

that booming self-assurance that tends to cost parents at least £20,000 a year. He was on his way to see a man routinely described by parliamentary sketch writers as 'Two Brains', and summed up by the *Guardian* as 'symbolic of a type of Tory that has come to prominence over the past twenty years – young, earnest, pious, confident: in a word, insufferable'.

This might sound a little overblown, but it's true: in a flash, that intuitive, visceral, aching Tory-hatred that had taken root during the Thatcher years rose up like a sudden fever. Had Mr Blair materialised right then, put his hand around my shoulder and said, 'I know you don't like a lot of what I do, but come on – we can't have *them* back, eh?', I would have probably nodded frantically and pledged undying allegiance.

That day, however, I was meeting someone who would do their best to disabuse me of all that unthinking tribalism. On the condition that we talk off the record – that is to say, I leave my tape recorder in my bag and frantically take notes – a serving Labour MP who was also an ex-minister had agreed to spend an hour talking to me about the government and its possible fate at the next election. I knew that this ex-minister would express biting dissent, and perhaps acknowledge the fact that voting Labour now seemed so counter-intuitive that the party all but deserved to suffer heavy electoral losses – but what was actually said went way beyond any of that.

The ex-minister talked, in pained terms, about the way that Mr Blair's tenure as leader had seen a change not just in the Labour Party's structures and processes, but in the simple way in which its senior members related to one another. 'The party used to be like a family. There were disagreements, but there was a warmth to the way we interacted.' My host's face screwed into a grimace. 'Now it's very *nasty*. A lot of the time, it's downright unpleasant.'

'All our traditions are breaking down,' the ex-minister went on. 'At the 2002 conference, I was heartened by what happened: the party's voting on Iraq, when there was an anti-Blair majority split 60/40 between those who insisted on UN backing for military action, and those who disapproved of military action no matter what. I thought, "This is the party I love." But it didn't count for anything – because Tony's way of running the party is to dismiss everything it does.'

Wilfully cut off from the party, rattled by the unending bad news from Iraq, Blair and his allies were, it seemed, palpably confused as to how to step back onto even ground. The consequences, among other things, included sporadic – and very Blairite – policy initiatives, the latest in the line that had begun with the evocation of drunken toughs being frogmarched to cash machines (July 2000), taken in a short-lived rhetorical crusade against the anti-social menace of chewing gum (October 2003), and would, by May 2004, lead to the suggestion that the brewers should somehow meet some of the costs of drunken behaviour. The latter, as with its predecessor, has not been heard of since.

'There's a lot of Emperor's New Clothes kind of thinking at the moment,' the ex-minister said. 'They all have a little mutter from time to time, and you hear declarations of some new strategy: like, "Time to draw a line under the Iraq war and move on." Or you'll hear a lot of "He'll turn it round. He's the great persuader." A lot of them are scared, but you've got to factor in this ruthless, domineering leadership, who keep thinking everything will get back to normal . . . But look at the policy initiatives we've had lately. Chewing gum wardens. Random drug testing in schools. They're like the kind of policies you got in the last days of John Major. And then there's this proposal that no sixteen-year-olds will leave school. They're trying to make that sound like a progressive policy, but it sounds like it will amount to extension of the mess that already exists: more targets, more student debt.'

And so we arrived at the possible results of the next election. The best outcome for the country, said the ex-minister, would be no outright majority, and a Labour–Liberal coalition without Mr Blair, who would have 'lost such face that he'd go anyway'. In this scenario – rendered slightly improbable by Charles Kennedy's repeated ruling-out of any hypothetical deal with the Lib Dems – the Prime Minister would, of course, be Gordon Brown, whose ascendancy might not quite represent the sea-change Labour's dissenters were after, but whose political path would be shaped by the circumstances of his accession.

Power-sharing, according to this argument, could result in electoral reform, a tilt away from the kind of illiberalism championed by Mr Blunkett, a shift in foreign policy, and, with any luck, a lasting change to the brain-dead, regimented ways of the House of Commons: 'You'd get away from that sense of things just being pushed through by an all-powerful government – because at the moment, the whole system has just broken down.' Even without the arrival of coalition politics, a scaled-down Labour majority would surely increase the leverage of the party's malcontents and result in at least some of these changes coming to pass.

My next question cut to the quick. In the context of all that, what would the ex-minister recommend to a disaffected Labour voter in a constituency held by an arch-Blairite with the Liberal Democrats running second?

The reply sounded a dramatic note indeed. 'I would recommend that you vote Liberal. For the sake of Labour's values and the future of the party, a correction has to take place.'

So there it was: heresy, plain and simple. Aside from my qualms about voting for the Lib Dems on account of the fact that many of them didn't seem to deserve it ('So what should you do?' raged the ex-minister. 'Vote Blair because you think Charles Kennedy might be as bad?'), the advice begged one question so obvious that I blurted it out without even thinking. The argument for voting Liberal Democrat so as to nudge a Labour-led government away from Blairism was based on one key supposition: the impossibility of the Tories managing to seize power. What if droves of Labour dissidents, giddy with the possibility of reclaiming the party as their own, split the progressive vote, and allowed Michael Howard to fly into Downing Street?

'The chances of Michael Howard getting into Downing Street are still very low,' said the ex-minister. 'There's room for a protest vote.'

There was a pause. 'And why don't we like Michael Howard? Partly because of his right-wing record when he was Home Secretary. But *we're* more right-wing than Michael Howard was: detail-for-detail, that was the case under Straw, and it's been even more like that with Blunkett. Okay, we've got something close to full employment, and increased spending on education and health – but the Tories now say they'll match it. I'm not saying I want the Tories, but how bad would it be? The thing is, the Labour Party needs a fright.'

This was dangerous talk, of course: precisely the kind of argument that sends Mr Blair and his colleagues into irate warnings about the dark days of the 1980s and those ill-advised people who always preferred the infantile purity of opposition to the adult world of government. It seemed far too trigger-happy, making light of the dreadful possibility of the Tories taking power. Could you really look at a modern Tory Cabinet – Howard taking the world stage, David Davis installed at the Home Office, the pretty odious Liam Fox in there somewhere – and shrugglingly ask whether, relatively speaking, it was really that bad?

Whatever, given the alleged unlikeliness of the Tories gaining power, the ex-minister's proposed 'fright' was aimed at affecting a Labour-led government. Ideally, it would result in not only a change of leader, but also a revival of the Labour Party outside Parliament, keen to ensure that it reaffirmed its influence over those at the top, lest they should ever drift away again. And on this score, of course, it wasn't very clear whether there was any great likelihood of such a back-to-the-roots revival taking place. One recent conference, the ex-minister said, had been redolent of a 'Nuremberg rally'; what was left of the Labour Party seemed to have long since adjusted to a life of meek obedience. 'The base may have shrivelled. That's what happened to the Tories post-Thatcher, and we're sort of going there. And then the question becomes whether there's really any party left to renew.'

The alternative – more likely, in all honesty – was a future under the same 'strangulated management' that characterised New Labour: preferable to the eternal reign of the Blairites, but perhaps only just. 'Gordon's much more Labour than Tony, and he really cares about social justice and poverty,' said the ex-minister, 'but he's just as bad a control freak. And he's a very pro-American Atlanticist. Where I start from is the need to get rid of Blair. That's the primary issue. And yes, Gordon is the only successor. So you take the best available option.'

At that point, a bell rang. Mustering up dwindling reserves of party loyalty, the ex-minister went off to troop obediently through the lobbies.

As the subsequent weeks went by and I shared the company of other Labour dissidents, it became more and more clear that the ex-minister's prescription for the party's ills marked them down as a lonely voice indeed. No matter how fretful they were about the Blairite project, even when they feared that his period in government might have left the party in ruins, none of the people I spoke to would be shaken from the idea that as long as there was a Labour Party, it was unthinkable not to vote for it. Even Tony Benn, a man whose political affinity with New Labour surely scores a zero, seemed to be having none of the suggestion that, if only as a way of kicking the party back into line, a non-Labour vote was worth considering. I sent him an interview-requesting email which mentioned the book's title; his reply was wonderfully curt. 'Please excuse,' he wrote. 'My interest is in reclaiming the Labour Party.'

Mere votes, however, would play no role in any imagined socialist renaissance. The advice I received from some of the party's most high-profile refuseniks was, in crudely reductive terms, to grit my teeth and carry on voting Labour – because it would at least stop Mr Howard sinking his fangs into our lives, and with any luck, they and their comrades might soon boot the Blairites out. Obviously, this wasn't all that satisfactory: a big

Labour vote at the next election would surely be hailed as a solid endorsement of Mr Blair and his works, and – even if Gordon Brown eventually lumbered into Downing Street – thereby might reduce the chances of much being put right.

All this came into focus when I met Peter Kilfoyle, the imposing MP – 'burly' really isn't the half of it – for the Liverpool constituency of Walton. Anyone who has followed the Blair government's recurrent tumbles into mishap will be at least vaguely familiar with Mr Kilfoyle: a rather grave, boomy-voiced presence, he is frequently summoned to TV and radio studios to issue critical verdicts on the government that (1) always stop short of outright mutiny (the closest he got was in the wake of 2004's local and Euro elections, when he told the BBC that the Prime Minister would have to 'decide whether he is an electoral asset or a liability'), and (2) are suffused by the noble sense of someone speaking for the Labour Party's long-forgotten proletarians. Had John Prescott been gifted with a higher IQ and opposed New Labour rather than embracing it, he and Mr Kilfoyle would probably pass for brothers.

His stripped-down personal history goes something like this: one of fourteen children born to impoverished Irish parents, he made it to Durham University before successfully battling with our old friends the Trotskyists as a Labour Party regional organiser, taking his seat in Parliament in 1991, and going on to sign Tony Blair's leadership nomination papers and take a role in his campaign. There followed the golden new dawn of 1997, after which he took on ministerial jobs in the Cabinet Office and Ministry of Defence. Latterly, surmising that New Labour was neglecting the needs of hard-bitten communities like Walton, and presumably chewing over whether assisting the Prime

Minister's ascendancy had been such a good idea, he returned to the backbenches.

Naturally enough, Mr Blair crept into just about everything we talked about: sometimes as an implied presence, often as the specific subject of our conversation – as when I wondered whether being so central to his early progress was a source of bitter regret. 'That's gone,' said Mr Kilfoyle, slightly wistfully. 'At the time, we were all preoccupied with getting a Labour government elected, we were shocked by the death of John Smith, and we knew that in '97 we had to win to maintain the party. That process hasn't stopped yet: we're still fighting for the resurrection of the party I knew. But I've no regrets. To me, he fitted the bill in terms of – ironically – presentation. What I never quite understood was just how convinced he was of his own rectitude in those matters of policy and party organisation, which were totally at odds with what I believed in. But that's history.'

He shared his thoughts in an uncomfortably smoky room, filled with an ever-increasing fug from his Benson and Hedges. The conversation was broken and stilted; built on impressive surges that would take shape, roar into life, and clearly point to a particular conclusion – usually, the toppling of the Prime Minister – only to recede into a vocabulary of caution and equivocation. At certain points, Mr Kilfoyle made me feel as if I was invading the Labour Party's privacy, by asking questions about subjects that were best left to him and his colleagues. 'We have our own processes for dealing with leadership,' he said at one point, when I asked if it was time to find somebody new. 'We're very loyal to our leaders.'

When I asked him how he would like the government's policies to change, however, it soon became clear that Peter Kilfoyle was on the right side of the argument. 'I believe in internationalism, for example,' he explained. 'I am not averse, in extremis, to military action: if your country's attacked, you defend yourself. What I do object to is tying our foreign policy to another country's objectives, when they are entirely irrelevant to what we, as a country, aspire to. What happened in Iraq was all about maintaining a fictitious special relationship.'

And so he went on (and he really did: one verbal splurge instantly followed another). 'If I deal with Foundation Hospitals, I don't like the idea of setting hospital against hospital. I don't believe in that kind of market solution to improving public services. And I particularly take exception to a process whereby these things are introduced out of thin air without going through all of the normal channels of debate.

'When you talk about high-quality healthcare at the point of need, that's free – that's *not* the direction we're going in. And I don't want to mortgage the flexibility of future administrations through PFIs. I don't even believe they're cost-effective. What I do want is the kind of investment in essential public services that leaves them in the public domain and not in private hands. Simply because, with a private operator, the bottom line is profit. That's it, full stop. I think we should aspire to something more for our public services. There's no profit in giving healthcare away free, is there?'

When he looked ahead to the next Labour manifesto, he seemed yet more concerned. At the time of our meeting, the Blairite vanguard were working themselves into a lather about the fashionable idea of Localism: à la Foundation Hospitals, somehow taking all kinds of public services out of the traditional government structures and 'empowering local communities to take control through genuine citizenship and genuine owner-ship' (the words are from *Communities in Control*, a slim Fabian Society pamphlet authored by Hazel Blears).

Mr Kilfoyle, by contrast, was not impressed. 'If you take a con-cept like Localism, where you put things down as far as you can, and people argue at the lowest level for their own immediate area, the people who are going to be advantaged by that are not the people in the sink estates – it's going to be articulate, profes-sional middle-class people,' he seethed. 'And you may say, well, what's changed? Well frankly, not a lot. If you read the *Daily Mail*, of course, you'd think there was some kind of assault on middle-class values, which I just don't recognise at all.'

A little over-enthusiastically, I jumped in. You must aspire to a change of the Labour leadership then, I said. You're certainly going to need massive changes in the upper reaches of the party if you're going to pull off the kind of shifts you're talking about.

'I aspire to a change of *thinking* in the party,' he advised, dis-appointingly. 'Leaderships can only operate within a collective mindset. I'd like to see a change in the thinking that has given rise to what I consider to be a political cul-de-sac. For the simple reason that, if we talk about the delivery of public services, I don't believe that the direction in which we're going will deliver the outcomes that we all want.'

Thinking back to my furtive encounter with the ex-minister, I changed tack. Even if we left the small matter of the Labour Party's top job aside, the kind of leftward jump that he was after wouldn't come about without a big electoral shock, would it?

He sounded almost helpless. 'I don't know,' he said. 'I really don't know.'

*

It was perhaps indicative of either ludicrous optimism or very muddled thinking that one of Mr Kilfoyle's proposed remedies for the Labour Party's malaise was a joint enterprise he was about to undertake with Stephen Byers, the almost comically Blairite ex-Secretary of State for Transport, Local Government and the Regions, who had recently crash-landed in the newspapers' political coverage on account of apparent ideas he was mooting for a third Labour term (many based around the New Labour totems of choice and – you've guessed it – Localism). Mr Kilfoyle was a little vague on the detailed plans for this mind-boggling double act, save for their shared wish to discover 'how we can regenerate enthusiasm for politics generally, and specifically Labour Party politics.'

No matter how great their differences, he said, both he and Mr Byers believed that they had the same general objectives, 'in accord with our values and principles'. That, as far as I could tell, bordered on the delusional – but it was a telling indicator of the the strange contortions that arose from attempting to redeem a Labour Party that might have passed into the political beyond. Indeed, pushed to the limits in his attempts to convince people like me to have faith while keeping himself within the party's big tent, there was only one mantra he could repeat. 'I say, "Vote Labour",' he said. 'Full stop. I assume that if the candidate is endorsed by the party, it's a Labour candidate.'

He couldn't really say anything else, of course. 'I think the electoral process is obviously the determining element, not only in who forms a government, but to a large extent, the nature of the government,' he went on. 'But that's not the only element. There are lots of other things. Public opinion has to be taken note of: it's been public opinion that's driven down the Prime

Minister's personal standing over Iraq. Obviously there have been politicians – mainly of his own party, I hasten to add – who have led the charge on that particular issue, but it's mainly been public opinion.'

The upshot of this was a little unclear. Was the only permissible thing to obediently vote Labour and then kick up a stink about a great deal of what they did? Elect a Blair government and then carry on marching against it?

'I'm not going to say, to *anybody*, that you don't vote Labour, for God's sake,' he said, tetchily. 'What I'm going to say is what I believe: that the worst of Labour governments is preferable to the best Tory governments. They're your options. And I don't think this is the worst of Labour governments. I think it's made major faux-pas, and it's got problems that we have to resolve internally, but I don't think that it's been tremendously bad.'

Okay, I thought. Let's try another tack. Do you think it would be beneficial to the Labour Party if the leverage of people like you was increased by its parliamentary majority being slightly smaller?

'Not necessarily. When you say leverage, I'm not after leverage. What I would like to see is change.'

This was now getting a bit surreal. You don't, I suggested, get political change without any leverage.

'It depends how you define leverage, I suppose,' he said. 'What would happen in the scenario that you propose . . . For example, if you have a majority of 167 or 173, you know that you can get what you want through the Commons. But if you have a majority of, say, 21 or so, which Major had, then you've got to do a lot more work to maintain your majority. That's a matter of simple mathematics.'

Had our conversation been represented in an animated cartoon, a lightbulb would suddenly have materialised above my head. Right, I said. And that kind of scenario would promote the kind of back-to-the-grassroots kind of thinking that you hold dear.

'It has to do. *Has to do.*'

So, a reduced Labour Party majority would be a good thing?

'I want to see as many Labour Members returned as I can.'

Well, the thing is, I said, those two positions are completely inconsistent.

'Perhaps,' he said, slightly mystically. 'But politics is inconsistent.'

And that was pretty much how we left our discussion: unresolved, inconclusive, shot through with all the illogical compromises and awkward accommodations that tend to come from a very British combination of big parties, Middle-English hegemony and the first-past-the-post electoral system. For good and all, I suspected, Mr Kilfoyle's political instincts would always be prevented from reaching their natural conclusions by the company that he thought he was forced to keep. It surely made for an awkward, frustrating kind of life; maybe that was why he smoked so much.

At least once, however, he had evidently been unable to keep it all in. As I was putting on my coat, I noticed a solitary Post-it note, balanced on a pile of papers to his left. In the kind of scrawl that suggested a sudden burst of anger, it said, 'Bugger New Labour'.

On 24 June 2001, the *Observer* published a comment article by Roy Hattersley headlined 'It's No Longer My Party'. The ex-deputy Labour leader – who stepped down as an MP in 1997 –

usually writes with an eloquence that lends his views a graceful kind of authority, though on this occasion his words also oozed a real sense of gravitas, as if he was writing about a development of truly epochal importance. They rather reminded me, in fact, of one of the speeches that peppered my O-level history textbooks: Lloyd George railing against the House of Lords, say, or Stanley Baldwin bemoaning the power of the press. 'Now my party not only pursues policies with which I disagree; its whole programme is based on a principle I reject,' he thundered. 'One thing is clear: I cannot retain both membership and self-respect unless I make apparent that much of what the Labour Party now proposes is wrong.'

Some of his ire was focused on a raft of policies: protection of the UK's remaining grammar schools, legal reforms which squashed civil liberties, the expansion of PFI. Far more important, however, was his underlying accusation that New Labour was following a credo that lay in complete opposition to the party's age-old emphasis on equality.

Mr Blair had long been in the habit of extolling the virtues of 'meritocracy', as if this social model – of the intelligent and able rising to the top, finally liberated from the stifling effects of class – was the embodiment of the ideal of fairness that he held so dear. 'The new Britain is a meritocracy where we break down the barriers of class, religion, race and culture,' he boasted to a 1997 meeting of Commonwealth heads of government. In one of his opening speeches in the 2001 campaign, he proudly claimed that, 'We are not old-style socialists. We are what we believe in. We are meritocrats.'

As Mr Hattersley pointed out, the M-word denoted a society that could be just as unequal as any system of inherited privilege: a vision of shifting patterns of inequality in which the poor would largely remain poor, and the rich could crow more loudly than ever about their justly-acquired fortunes. Worse still, he wrote, 'to add to the unfairness, characteristics which enable the "meritorious" to succeed are made more visible by a middle-class upbringing'. Thus, the idea of social mobility on which the idealised meritocracy was based was, 'to most of the children of the inner cities, a cruel joke'.

Now, given Mr Blair's rather dilettantish approach to all kinds of concepts – the Third Way, Communitarianism, the Stake-holder Society – it could perhaps be countered that the Prime Minister was advocating a benign reading of an idea whose harsher aspects he didn't actually understand. Unfortunately, too many of his policies had suggested meritocracy in full, cruel effect: his resistance to increasing the top rates of income tax, his advocacy of schools that could select some of their pupils on the basis of 'aptitude', his conviction that we are usually best off allowing our affairs to be decided through the machinations of the market.

I read the *Observer* article through a hungover fog at a jazz festival near Lichfield. I was sufficiently moved, however, to phone some of my old Labour Party compadres and marvel at both the severity of the attack and its unlikely author. Back when we had spent rain-sodden evenings sticking leaflets through letterboxes and Hattersley was the deputy Labour leader (as Shadow Chancellor, his underlings had included the young Tony Blair), he was held to be the kind of washed-out right-winger at whom it was the done thing to sneer; Neil Kinnock, by contrast, dispensed the kind of incendiary rhetoric that kept us warm. Now Kinnock was cloistered in Brussels as a European Commissioner, issuing occasional comments on the British political scene that suggested he had long since become a Blair apologist. By contrast, Hattersley's article suggested his own version of Tony Benn's claim that he had 'left Parliament to go into politics'. And so he has gone on: his weekly *Guardian* column often amounts to reassuring proof that there is still a corner of the Labour Party that has not gone potty.

After a brief flurry of emails, I met Mr Hattersley – aka Baron Hattersley of Sparkbrook – in his cramped office, perched atop a building near Covent Garden. That lunchtime, Mr Blair had stood in front of the Commons and announced his volte-face on a referendum on the European constitution. 'He was marvellous today,' said Mr Hattersley. 'If only he was a socialist.' When I recalled my meeting with Hazel Blears, his face broke into a irreverent smirk. 'When I was told that Hazel Blears was now in charge of security policy,' he smiled, 'all I could think of was that line from *Dad's Army*: "We're doomed, we're all doomed."'

I shared an hour or so of Mr Hattersley's time when excited newspaper and television chatter about the supposedly imminent succession of Gordon Brown was starting to reach its peak. That possibility, which duly receded into the middle distance, informed a good deal of what he said, though the likelihood or otherwise of the Chancellor striding into Number 10 would not alter his key bit of advice to the millions of distressed Labour supporters with whom he sympathised. In essence, his message was this: a successor would arrive one day, and in the meantime – partly to safeguard the party that Blair's replacement would inherit – we had to carry on putting our crosses in the same old box.

That day, he had taken lunch with the Education Secretary Charles Clarke – who, he said, had claimed that successfully nudging the UK towards the heart of Europe remained Mr Blair's most treasured aim. In turn, that contention coloured Mr Hattersley's mapping of the next two or three years. In the ideal scenario, he said, Labour would win the next election with a majority of 50 or 60, call a referendum on the EU constitution, and – if Blair and his allies finally stated the case for it – defeat Michael Howard, Robert Kilroy-Silk, Joan Collins and the Eurosceptic hordes. Having thus achieved his long-standing aim of cementing Britain's European destiny, Mr Blair might then resign – whereupon Gordon Brown would reconnect the government to the Labour Party, acknowledge the fact that the fires of socialist orthodoxy were still burning bright, and gently call time on the New Labour project.

If all that seemed to be based on wishful thinking – not least the idea that the government might somehow win the referendum – it at least shed light on Mr Hattersley's key conviction: he wanted rid of Blair and Blairism, and he took heart from the fact that the end might just be in sight. (A few months later, of course, the aspect of his argument dealing with the length of the Prime Minister's tenure, if not the shelf-life of his ideas, was given the ring of truth by Blair's retirement announcement.) Moreover, whereas plenty of hardened cynics might claim that the Prime Minister's most likely successor would simply prolong the New Labour project, Mr Hattersley had grounds for cautious optimism.

'I know that if we'd had Gordon's way, instead of having top-up fees, we'd have had a graduate tax,' he said. 'That's a big difference. I know that if we'd had Gordon's way, we wouldn't have had Foundation Hospitals. Now, I'm not suggesting that Gordon will become Prime Minister and he'll announce the abolition of those things, but at least there won't be any more drift in that direction. When Gordon Brown becomes leader, as I believe he will, he'll be very much like Labour leaders I've known in the past. It won't end the argument about where the Labour Party goes, but it'll move us one step in the right direction.'

And so we reached the most crucial point. If this sea-change was to occur, wavering Labour supporters would have to bury their misgivings and once again do the right thing. In most cases, Mr Hattersley claimed, this would not represent quite the teeth-grindingly counter-intuitive action it might suggest: 'The parliamentary party is, now and always, utterly craven,' he said. 'If Robin Cook were to become leader on Thursday, a majority of the parliamentary Labour Party would be Cookites.' Even those who were unlucky enough to have to vote for the likes of Sîon Simon or Hazel Blears could apparently take heart: like so many apparent Blairite monsters, they could be reasonably expected to eventually change their spots.

All that apart, there was no sense to the aforementioned ex-minister's claim that the Labour Party would be best served by the delivering of a big electoral fright. 'I don't believe that,' said Mr Hattersley, emphatically. 'I don't think political parties ever improve with failure. Blair and Blairism are a result of failure. If we hadn't failed for eighteen years, we wouldn't be where we are now – we'd have a genuinely socialist, democratic party. So I don't want there to be any kind of bloody nose.'

Mr Blair, it seemed, was fortunate to have such reasonable enemies. 'I have no wish for the Prime Minister to be ejected,' he continued. 'I don't want a palace coup, I don't want a political assassination – I want him to go in his own good time, in his own way, because too many Labour administrations have ended in chaos, and I don't want that to happen to this one. I want there to be a peaceful transition. But when the change comes, the overwhelming likelihood is that the new leader will be somebody who operates within Labour Party terms. That doesn't mean I'll agree with everything a new Labour leader does, but the argument will return to Labour parameters. At the moment, it's outside them.'

There were big caveats to all this, of course. For example, those of us who were appalled by the onward march of PFI would probably have to adjust to the fact that our arguments would always founder against all those sparkling new hospitals and schools. 'You and I are on the side of the complicated argument,' he explained, 'and socialism *is* a complicated argument, and it's very difficult to put over against these clichés like "I've no time for ideology, I just want what works."'

Even so, despite Iraq and tuition fees and creeping privatisation, he could confidently state the case for the government that he had so often opposed. 'They've done a number of very positive things that you and I can endorse,' he advised. 'They have a wonderful record on primary education, the minimum wage, in dealing with the working poor – there are a number of things we can boast about, and I will boast about come the election. And the Labour Party remains the only possible vehicle for achieving the ideals which I have. If there's ever going to be a vehicle for egalitarianism in this country, that's it. So the best you can do is hang on: this government are better than the others, it's done a lot of good things – and what's more, it remains a strong possibility, perhaps a strong *probability*, that we can get it back on track one day.

'There's no alternative,' he insisted. 'The Liberals won't do it; there's no point in forming a new party. But the idea of equality will remain. And the Labour Party is the best possible vehicle for it.'

If that conviction seemed reasonable enough, there were times when Mr Hattersley sounded like one of those Christians who can survey a world of war and pestilence and surmise that somehow God's plan is still intact, and the glorious day of judgement will soon arrive. As he watched the meritocratic dystopia taking root and heard the lonely echo of his often solitary voice, where did he get his optimism from?

'It's partly psychological,' he admitted, with a grin, 'because I am optimistic by nature. If there is a golden age, it is in the future, not in the past. And part of it is, I think the idea of equality is so strong, that in the end it will break through. I have a great faith, and this may be irrational optimism, in what is right and true prevailing in the end. *Magnus est veritas, et prevalebit* – you know the Latin text?'

I didn't, actually. But even if I ruled out his imagined socialist Second Coming, he could still advocate one persuasive reason for voting Labour: the awful, chilling, flatly apocalyptic prospect of the first Conservative victory since 1992. The ex-minister had claimed that the differences between New Labour and Michael Howard *et al* might turn out to be academic; Mr Hattersley, predictably enough, was having none of it.

'They would be vastly different,' he fumed. 'First of all, they wouldn't spend as much on public services. It's no good pretending that they'd concentrate their spending on health and education: when difficulties come along, and difficulties will come along, their instinct will be to cut spending. I think their education policies are quite different: the idea that they're going to break down catchment areas is the beginnings of it; I think we'd get very near to going back to selection. I think their health policy – it's going to be two tiers with some of our hospitals, but it becomes three tiers with them, because they'd enable people to use their health service vouchers. So it would be much worse. Very, very much worse.'

And so he reached his conclusion, dispensed when I asked him what he would say to a lifelong Labour voter who was thinking of sending the leadership of the party a message by voting for the Liberal Democrats.

'I'd say they were wasting their time and their vote,' he said, conjuring up a sternness and impatience that had so far failed to materialise. 'Because the next election, like every election in my lifetime, is between the Labour Party and the Conservative Party. In May 2005, you and I – well, not me, because I don't have a vote – but you and a number of other people are going to have to decide who you want: *Tony Blair or Michael Howard*.'

4 Schools

'Effectively managing change with experienced change managers'

The day of last year's local and European elections, I drove from my home in the Wye Valley to West Yorkshire, initially through that verdant corridor on the English–Welsh borders that takes in Leominster, Church Stretton, Craven Arms and Ludlow. The route – along the A49 – has yet to sprout many dual carriageways; instead, it winds mesmerically through the kind of small towns where kids still go halves on ten cigarettes and Sundays take on a very English sense of comfortable tedium.

The number of UKIP posters tacked to fences and trees suggested that this was staunch Euro-sceptic country (and so it proved: the party finished third in the West Midlands constituency, nearly four points ahead of the Lib Dems), an impression bolstered by the fact that, with the European football Championship looming, so many houses displayed both UKIP hoardings and the flag of St George. In tandem, they seemed colours flown not in celebration of an English ideal, but in a paranoid defensiveness, born of the kind of headlines regularly smeared over the pages of the *Sun*, *Mail* and *Express*.

One of the prevailing myths of modern Britain is that our national life is under dire threat from an invasive coalition of Eurocrats, metropolitan trendies and asylum-seekers; given UKIP's ascent, and the Conservatives' sympathy with that kind of worldview, it seems certain to colour the next election. It's a shame, because a whole raft of forces *are* conspiring to snuff out some of the UK's most treasured traditions – though UKIP and the Conservatives (and New Labour, come to think of it) probably wouldn't recognise the problem.

Bradford, where I was first headed, has some claim to being the birthplace of public education. The 1870 Education Act, which empowered local councils to provide education, was introduced to Parliament by William Forster, a Bradford MP. In the 1890s, the Christian Socialist Margaret McMillan began a successful campaign to make Bradford's school authorities install bathrooms, improve ventilation and contribute to the feeding of their pupils, setting out on a path that would lead to the 1906 Provision of School Meals Act.

The early twenty-first century had placed Bradford in the vanguard of a slightly less noble enterprise. As of early 2001, as part of a drive towards what was termed 'LEA Outsourcing', the running of Bradford's Local Education Authority had been handed to Serco, a multinational firm who also saw to the operation of the Docklands Light Railway, HM Prison Dover, hundreds of speed cameras, the RAF early-warning station at Fylingdales in North Yorkshire, and a bus company in Adelaide, Australia. Their range of interests made for good business: in 2001, they announced an annual turnover of over £1 billion, and profits of £46.4 million.

You don't read much about them, but such companies – characterised by nondescript logos, a fondness for corporate jargon, and websites featuring grinning people in hard hats – are as integral a part of modern Britain as government special advisers and management consultants. During the research for this book, I became oddly fascinated by them; in my darker moments, I had *Blade Runner*-esque visions of a future in which their insignia flash from every building within eyeshot and the wearing of their polo shirts becomes compulsory.

Though such images are the stuff of paranoid fantasy (for the time being, at least), the rash of LEA Outsourcing that took place in 2000–2001 attests to the companies' clout: in addition to Serco's new role in Bradford, Nord Anglia ('Committed to high quality education services provision') were invited to take over LEAs in Hackney, Sandwell and Waltham Forest; Capita ('The UK's leading support services company') was preparing for work in Leeds and Haringey; and the construction company WS Atkins – for some reason – had decided to try its hand at education in Southwark.

The Bradford end of things had been observed by two people I met at the National Union of Teachers' local office: Ian Murch, the full-time Secretary of the Bradford branch, and Jane Rendell, a Maths teacher who puts in time as his assistant. Over tea and biscuits in their musty-smelling HQ, they told the story with an air of frustrated bafflement, presumably heightened by the fact that what had happened in Bradford had been the work of a Labour government. On occasion they would laugh at the lunacy of it all, though it made for a mirthless kind of sound.

The tale went something like this. In 2000, an Ofsted report on Bradford's Education Authority highlighted problems that were at least partly traceable to two factors: a troublesome reorganisation of its schools from a three-tier model – primary, middle and senior – into a conventional two-tier system, and low levels of academic achievement founded in the city's social make-up. Bradford, put simply, is a poor city with a disproportionately small middle class. In addition, its schools include large numbers of children with families from the Indian subcontinent, and in particular from rural Pakistan. 'We have probably the poorest community that comes from abroad in large numbers, any-where in Britain,' said Ian. 'In terms of educational understand-ing in the home, those things weigh heavily here.'

With rapier-like certainty – and suspicions of a stitch-up involving Bradford's City Council and the then Education Secretary Estelle Morris – the suggested solution to at least some of these problems was LEA Outsourcing. Thus commenced a bidding process, and the eventual awarding of a ten-year, £360 million contract, tied to the attainment of around 80 points of improvement, to Serco – who simply swallowed up most of the Education Authority's staff and blithely renamed their new divi-sion Education Bradford.

Serco had precious little experience of administering educa-tion in Britain, but it didn't seem to much bother them. 'They had no one with an educational background,' Ian told me. 'The man who came here to present their bid had been the Chief Education Officer for Bedfordshire. He had taken early retire-ment and been recruited to go around and bid for contracts on Serco's behalf. At the point at which they got the contract, he stopped working for them. He never came to work here – he was there to put together a credible bid and front it for them. And he was quite a plausible bloke. Big and affable.'

The initial response to the outsourcing idea had seen a spate of public meetings, and a rally outside the Town Hall. Bradford's Labour councillors remained pretty much silent; the ever-prag-matic Liberal Democrats said they would try to ensure that the new arrangements worked in the city's interests; the only party to join in the protests were the Greens. 'Most teachers, and most people, were completely baffled,' said Jane. 'Whenever there were public meetings, people said, "Look at the disaster that Railtrack has been – why are they doing this to our schools?" And look at how much more simple running Railtrack was than educating kids. That's what really astounded me. It was an output-specified contract; they thought that they could specify the outputs for education closely enough to get someone doing the job. And of course, it's much more complicated than that.'

Serco's formal proposal for the work they had been given was, perhaps not surprisingly, couched in a platitudinous management-speak, suggestive of a nightmare hybrid of Charles Clarke and David Brent. 'Schools should be the focal point for their communities – "Community hubs",' advised one passage. 'We will provide a management toolkit which has proved successful in our other businesses,' assured another. The most rib-tickling sentence ran as follows: 'We will add value to the services in the scope and beyond the scope of this project by effectively managing change with experienced change managers.' ('I remember our change manager,' said Ian. 'He was twenty-five. I don't think he'd seen much change.')

What such verbal sophistry served to conceal was a blunt approach to Bradford's finances. 'Pretty quickly, that was made very clear to us by the company,' said Ian. 'They were absolutely candid about it when they came in: they had bid to run the LEA for about 10 per cent less cost than it was being run for already. That was one of their big selling points. They also said that the company itself wanted a 5-to-10 ten per cent take from the turnover.'

Serco, in short, claimed to have such a masterful grasp of efficiency that it bordered on corporate magic: they would improve education in Bradford while cutting spending by between 15 and 20 per cent. Pretty quickly, the effects of all this became clear: a gradual erosion of the kind of jobs that lay outside the key target of upping exam results. By the summer of 2003, for example, the number of Bradford's educational psychologists – who work across a number of schools, supervising pupils with Special Needs – had dropped from twenty to ten. As evidenced by a slew of letters to the local press, among the most alarmed by this were parents whose children were dyslexic. 'The practical result of that,' said Jane, 'is that schools are left struggling with children who have very severe needs that the education psychologist would usually deal with, giving the kind of back-up you'd normally expect. Classroom teachers are being left to deal with problems that aren't properly analysed. Schools complain about that all the time.'

If those kind of reductions suggested a new emphasis on the tightening of Bradford's financial belt, other aspects of the city's new set-up suggested a reckless kind of profligacy. One of the most glaring lunacies of outsourced LEAs is the fact that, though a private company takes on an education authority's functions, a so-called Residual LEA – made up of senior council executives – remains in place to oversee the operation of the contract. You thus end up with two lots of senior management, some of whom are on six-figure salaries. In Bradford, the problem was hardly helped by Serco's habit of seeking to address some of the city's specific difficulties by appointing highly paid dedicated managers. 'If you go and look in the car park at Future House, where they're now based, there are a lot of expensive cars in there, which there never were in the old LEA,' said Ian. 'There's loads of big new 4x4s there now, because they've appointed a primary achievement manager, a secondary achievement manager, an inclusion manager.'

All of this had had one clear result: rather than scything through Bradford's budgets and neatly sealing off a handsome profit, Serco had got in the habit of simply asking for more money from the City Council. 'We had a wonderful thing last year,' said Ian. 'I sit on a thing called the Finance Strategy Group, which determines how the money that's available for education is shared out. And the Director of Education came to it with a list of things that money was needed for. One of them said, "Funding for Serco for carrying out extra work: one million pounds." We said, "That's a nice round sum, isn't it? What's it for?" He said, "I can't tell you because it's commercially confidential." We had a stand-off, so they had to back off and give us a series of headings. A lot of it was just, "This is costing us more than we thought when we got the contract."'

'The contract is uprated annually for inflation, by 3 per cent,' he continued. 'But they've come back, for each of the full two years they've done so far, and said, "This is nowhere near enough", and renegotiated it, putting in about a million pounds more each time. Also, the government has coughed up quite a lot more money which it's put into it to save face. And I reckon it's now costing more than the old LEA used to cost. We're delivering the level of services that we used to have, but it's now costing 10 or 15 per cent more.'

It might seem simplistic to trace much of that to the sudden need for a profit – but the figures fit handsomely. Moreover, if you're one of those parents whose Special Needs child has been left without much help, there would seem to be one obvious reading of your predicament: you're no longer getting the help you once did because Bradford's new educational overlords have to draw a dividend. Worse still, relative to Serco's initial plans, not that much has actually been delivered. By 2003, of the 80-odd points of improvement Serco had committed to work on, three-quarters of one of them had been fulfilled, thus earning them around one per cent of their achievement bonuses. As a result, that aspect of their deal with Bradford's council has also been renegotiated.

One episode from Serco's recent history in Bradford gave the tale a wonderful element of comic relief, while also shining light on the incongruity of fusing public service with standard corporate rituals – in this case, the foreign 'jolly'. One of the more unlikely items in Serco's portfolio is a contract to run schools in Barbados – and in October 2003, thirteen Bradford head teachers were flown to the Caribbean to have a look at their operation. The fact that a trip to rural Pakistan might have been more instructive did not seem to count for much: 'There is massive underachievement by Afro-Caribbean pupils nationally,' said a primary head teacher called Richard Liddington, 'and this is a way of developing positive role models among their community.' Mr Liddington, unfortunately, admitted that there was only one Afro-Caribbean pupil on the roll of his school.

Serco's contract in Bradford has seven years left to run, but the concept of LEA outsourcing is now starting to gather dust. In December 2002, of the nine LEAs that had outsourced services, five were rated as poor, and three as unsatisfactory. The following May, WS Atkins had its Southwark contract terminated two years early. The government, presumably on account of the policy's failures, has come up with new ideas for raising standards in allegedly struggling schools; the service companies, given their seemingly infinite expertise, seem to have no shortage of alternative projects.

Not long after I returned from Bradford, I decided to test the limits of their ambitions by typing 'Serco Iraq' into Google. On rebuild-iraq-expo.com, a site offering opportunities to companies who fancied clearing up after American and British forces, I found this:

> Serco, the support services group, has become one of the first British firms to win business in Iraq with a contract to restore air traffic control services to Baghdad and Basra airports. The management deal awarded by the US agency for international development is relatively small – less than £5 million a year – but it puts Serco in a better position to win other business there. Confirmation of the 18-month contract came as Serco claimed to be successfully 'exporting' Private Finance Initiative models abroad. It said that within five years, half of its business could come from overseas.

Reading that solitary paragraph gave rise to a sudden flash of anxiety. If the government's fondness for private finance made for such a seamless connection between the war in Iraq and New Labour's education policies, what surreal world were they busy creating?

A couple of weeks after I visited Bradford, I met Tracy Morton and Kay Wilkinson, two mothers from Conisbrough, a sometime mining community not far from Doncaster. They were engaged in a passionate fight against a formidable coalition of enemies that included the government, Doncaster's elected Labour mayor, and Sir Peter Vardy, a man recently described by the *Times Education Supplement* as a 'Christian fundamentalist car dealer'. Their battleground was a schools policy to which the government now pledges heartfelt allegiance: the replacement of 'bog standard comprehensives' with the gleaming new creations known as Academies.

We met in the Windmill Community Centre, a box-like construction built on one of Conisbrough's post-war council estates. Inside, nine or ten pensioners were splitting their time between a game of bingo and making tea in a small kitchen area at the back. Kay and Tracy, meanwhile, were going about their jobs as local youth workers, responsible for the pastoral care of some of the area's more troublesome kids: one of their charges maintained an awkward, glowering presence for fifteen minutes or so, until his parents arrived to pick him up.

Tracy and Kay both had high-achieving daughters at Northcliffe, a comprehensive school that served Conisbrough and nearby Denaby. Carly, Kay's eldest, was predicted to get a run of As at GCSE and was apparently set on becoming a barrister; Sophie, Tracy's thirteen-year-old, had begun to scale similar heights and was determined to make it to university. Both of them had benefited from Northcliffe's so-called Gifted and Talented programme: Carly was entered for some of her GCSEs a year early, and both she and Sophie took advantage of specially laid-on Saturday morning lessons.

If Tracy, Kay and their kids had good reason to feel positive about their school, officialdom had only seemed to back them up. In 2001, Northcliffe was inspected by Ofsted and credited with being 'a good and improving school'. Both that year and in 2002, the DfES gave Northcliffe a School Achievement Award ('developed to celebrate the achievements of schools that have either made significant improvement or are high performing', in the words of the Department's website). In 2003, the school's pupils produced the bests SATs and GCSE results in its history; despite being the most disadvantaged school in the control of Doncaster's LEA, Northcliffe thus finished in the middle of local league tables.

Three months later, however, Northcliffe was placed in Special Measures by the Schools Inspectorate – the category denotes a school which is 'failing or likely to fail to give its pupils an acceptable standard of education'. 'When we got the report, and we read it, we were just like, "What school are they on about?" said Kay. "Are they really on about Northcliffe?"'

'It was really contradictory,' said Tracy. 'On one hand, they were saying the head was providing good leadership, and he'd got the support and loyalty of his staff – which sounds like great leadership. But on the other hand, there were faults in his vision and forward planning. They said that the standard of teaching was too low; ridiculously low. Relative to two years previous, it just seemed to have plummeted. So it was quite a shock: it had just got its best ever GCSE results – and it was being put in Special Measures. I was stunned.'

Five months after that, Doncaster's LEA unveiled plans to replace Northcliffe with an Academy run by a charitable organisation called the Vardy Foundation. The announcement would perhaps have been best made via letters to local parents; instead, it came in the pages of the Doncaster *Free Press*. 'The idea was to catch the wave and say, "You've got a failing school, but look – we're going to give you 23 million pounds and a lovely new school,"' said Tracy. 'And a lot of people were like, "Wow – wonderful." But the paper was also canny enough to say the school would be run by evangelical Christian sponsors.'

Such was the second phase of the town of Doncaster's dalliance with one of Mr Blair's most remarkable allies. When reading the story below, it's useful to occasionally remind yourself that it's the tale of plans enacted by a Labour government, a Labour mayor, and a Labour-dominated local council. If you cling to the idea that, despite their various transgressions, the party's upper echelons remain committed to the kind of ideas that can broadly be termed progressive, you might find what follows very troubling indeed.

Academies, initially known as City Academies, were publicly rolled out in 2000 by David Blunkett, who aimed at using them to replace schools that were either in Special Measures or deemed to be 'underachieving'. Four years later, the government planted the idea at the core of its education platform for the General Election, announcing plans to open up to two hundred. The idea is roughly this: for a fee of £2 million – payable in random instalments – private benefactors are handed effective control of brand new state schools, although the taxpayer meets the lion's share of both building and running costs (which, the figures suggest, tends to involve an initial sum of at least £20 million, and annual payments of around £5 million). The relatively small size of their contribution has little bearing on the sponsors' clout: they can appoint the majority of the school's governors and thereby have the crucial say in the appointment of senior management, and shape the school's practices without having to worry about the national curriculum. Stranger still, Academies are not bound by national agreements on teachers' pay and conditions. Truly, this is the stuff that the occupants of boardrooms tend to term 'win/win'.

The government has an organisation to curry goodwill among

those who might be interested in getting involved: the Academy Sponsors Trust is chaired by the carpet magnate Philip Harris, the sometime Archbishop of Canterbury George Carey, and Lord Levy of Mill Hill, Blair's 'special envoy' in the Middle East and – thanks to his founding of Magnet Records – the man who brought the world 'Rockabilly Rebel' by Matchbox. Its inaugural dinner took place in October 2004, though several enthusiastic benefactors had obviously not needed to be schmoozed: among those already involved in Academies were Sir Frank Lowe, the sports agent who represents Anna Kournikova; Amey and the Tribal Group (two of New Labour's beloved service companies); and the Corporation of London, whose new school in Southwark would reportedly underline its educational ethos by having an entrance hall built around a huge digitised readout of the FTSE index.

Among those who had got in particularly early was Sir Peter Vardy, a millionaire car dealer and Christian evangelist from Durham. Under the auspices of the Thatcher government's not-entirely-dissimilar City Technology Colleges Programme, his Vardy Foundation, run by Vardy's brother David, had already seen to the opening of a school called Emmanuel College in Gateshead. Thanks to the City Academies initiative, September 2003 saw the arrival of a second school, the King's Academy in Middlesbrough. The following March, it was ceremonially opened by none other than Tony Blair, who was given a tour of the school and presented with a Middlesbrough FC shirt bearing his surname. Two weeks later, he enthused about his visit during Prime Minister's Question Time. 'There is nothing more inspiring,' he said, 'particularly when one knew the old school that the King's Academy replaced, than to see the brand new buildings, the total commitment of the teachers and staff, and the pupils there eager to learn.'

Both Vardy schools certainly lie some distance from the underachieving, anarchic stereotype with which the government recurrently maligns the old comprehensive ideal. Buttoned-up, disciplinarian, and characterised by an almost corporate efficiency, they outwardly suggest enviable success: every year since 1996, for example, Emmanuel College's GCSE results have placed it in the top twelve non-selective British state schools.

Unfortunately, that's only half the story. Peter Vardy's Christian beliefs are shared by John Burn, the sometime head of Emmanuel College and now Education Adviser to the Vardy Foundation, and Nigel McQuoid, the principal at the King's Academy. Papers the pair have co-authored give a flavour of the way they see their beliefs impacting on education: 'If relativist philosophy is acceptable, then sado-masochism, bestiality and self-abuse are to be considered as wholesome activities,' runs one. 'It is very important that young people begin to realise that activities which are "private and personal" often degrade oneself and are not necessarily good and acceptable.' By way of clarifying the latter position, Mr McQuoid recently told the *Observer* that 'the Bible says clearly that homosexual activity is against God's design. I would indicate that to young folk.'

Most notoriously, Vardy schools accord equal importance to both creationism and theories of evolution. According to Mr McQuoid, though state schools are required to teach evolutionary theory, 'also, schools should teach the creation theory as literally depicted in Genesis'. The three-hundred year reign of the enlightenment apparently counts for very little at all: in his view, creation and evolution are both 'faith positions'. Mr Blair, it should be noted, has claimed to have no problem with such a stance. In 2002, when asked by the Liberal Democrat MP Jenny Tonge if he was happy about creationism being taught alongside evolution in state schools, he replied: 'I am very happy. I know that the Hnourable Lady is referring to a school in the north-east [i.e., Emmanuel College], and I think that certain reports about what it has been teaching are somewhat exaggerated. It would be very unfortunate if concerns about that issue were seen to remove the very strong incentive to ensure that we get as diverse a school system as we properly can. In the end, a more diverse school system will deliver better results for our children.'

When it comes to the context in which non-scientific subjects should be taught, a document once posted on Emmanuel College's website (but subsequently removed) goes into a very revealing kind of detail. As far as art lessons are concerned, 'A Christian perspective would see the body as the Temple of the Holy Spirit. Therefore, in a study of Art History related to figure drawing skills, emphasis would be given to Leonardo, Dürer, Michelangelo and Rodin rather than current modern artists.' With reference to English Literature, the document haughtily advises against 'what is dull, drab, morally compromised and empty'. The section dealing with History, meanwhile, is truly mind-boggling. 'God intervened into [sic] History in the person of Christ,' it says, 'and He has the power to allow or frustrate man's aims. In this context, it becomes important to peruse why Hitler paused at the English Channel when an immediate invasion might have led to a swift victory. Could it be that God was calling a halt to this march of evil?' (i.e., the Almighty was perhaps alright with the killing of six million Jews, but maybe the invasion of Britain was a bridge too far).

In February 2004, there came yet more strange news. In Middlesbrough, the local press reported that the King's Academy had decided to purge its library of Harry Potter books. According to the Teesside *Morning Gazette*, 'staff were said to be worried about the series containing connotations of the occult and witchcraft'.

After Emmanuel College and the King's Academy, the Vardy Foundation – in concert with Doncaster's mayor, Martin Winter, and the town's borough council – had proposed the opening of a third school in Thorne, a small town twenty minutes' drive from Conisbrough. Government approval of the scheme arrived in January 2004: David Miliband, the Blairite schools minister, optimistically assured the *Yorkshire Post* that he was sure it would result in 'a successful and popular school [that] will do much to improve opportunities for the young people it serves'. The saga of the scheme's passage from proposal to confirmation, however, suggested that such rosy predictions were offset by altogether darker intrigue.

Thorne's existing comprehensive, Thorne Grammar – the name is a residue of its selection-era origins – had spent two years in the Ofsted category known as Serious Weaknesses, applied to schools 'deemed to have significant weaknesses in one or more areas which need to be addressed but which are providing an acceptable standard of education overall'. In the wake of significant improvements, it was taken out of that bracket in early 2003 – but soon after, Doncaster's authorities nonetheless announced a proposal to close the school, and open a Vardy Academy on the same site. The plan was couched in terms of a golden chance for an embattled, underachieving community: nothing less than 'a unique opportunity to raise the aspirations and achievements of future generations'.

One month before the announcement, Dr Tony Brookes, Thorne Grammar's head, had resigned, under pressure from Doncaster's Director of Education. An industrial tribunal subsequently found that he had been made the victim of 'insidious' pressure and therefore unfairly dismissed – but in the meantime, his exit appeared to play the authorities an ace. Plenty of people I met in Yorkshire reckoned that he would have capably led opposition to the Academy plan; now, a potentially troublesome voice had been safely marginalised. 'I have felt very hurt by the way it has been done,' Dr Brookes later reflected, 'but the pressure at the time was enormous. I was told it was best to retire rather than go through any more anguish. They clearly wanted me out, and it's now emerging why.'

The local consultation process was squeezed into less than a month, taking in a spate of meetings between staff, parents and interested Thorne residents and representatives of both Doncaster Council and the Vardy Foundation. A one-page 'questionnaire' was also distrubuted, which featured no mention of the Vardy Foundation, and only two sentences: 'I support the proposal to establish an Academy in Thorne' (followed by boxes labelled 'Agree strongly', 'Agree', 'Disagree', and 'Disagree strongly'), and 'I have the following additional comments'. Little more than seventy were sent back to the council, who subsequently announced that 87 per cent of their respondents supported the plan.

Some of Thorne Grammar's teachers got the distinct impression that they were witnessing the enactment of a *fait accompli*. 'There wasn't a consultation process as I would understand it,' one of them told me. 'At the meetings, we were allowed to ask questions with no comeback, and that was it. There were no votes, no ballot papers. *Nothing*. I actually asked the people from the LEA, "How do you assess whether or not we accept this?" They said, "Well, we judge the kind of response we get from the meetings." There was never a real way of registering any dissent. And anyway, we were operating in the dark: a lot of people didn't even know what academies *were*. The sort of questions that we had were probably not very well-focused, because it was all completely new.'

Still, they tried. Enquiries to the Vardy Foundation people about their stance on creationism and evolution were met with predictably evasive answers: 'They said, "Well, we teach both. Creationism's *right*, but we do consider the other idea."' When it came to questions about the Foundation's reasons for extending their operations into South Yorkshire, the teachers were assured that they wanted do so according to the most honourably philanthropic motives (in the words of their own publicity blurb, they claimed to be 'a Northern family trust investing in your children's future'). Representatives of Doncaster's LEA, meanwhile, were asked what would happen if the plan foundered, and Thorne Grammar remained: would they seek to improve the school with the same zeal they were applying to the Vardy proposal? 'When that came up,' my teacher contact told me, 'the LEA basically said, "If that happens, you're on your own." And that, of course, rang alarm bells.'

By June 2003, Doncaster's authorities had drawn the consultation process to a close. Local people, according to a council spokesman, had 'been given ample opportunity to voice any concerns'. In vain, Dr Tony Brookes told local reporters that 'these plans have been swift, some might say too swift', and sounded a note of alarm about the Vardy Foundation's motives and bizarre beliefs: 'To me, they are using their £2 million input to buy into children's minds.' A local independent councillor named Martin Williams, however, was having none of it. 'This cannot be a bad thing for the area,' he said. 'As far as the religious aspect goes, I don't think it will be brainwashing the children. Pupils are intelligent enough to make up their own minds at that age.'

So it was that Thorne's 11-to-18-year-olds were inducted into a heavenly new era. In time, the Vardy Foundation circulated literature brimming with enthusiasm about the prospect of improved exam results and the new school's 'business and enterprise emphasis', but also serving notice of the Foundation's very individual approach to state-funded education. School mornings, they advised, would begin with 'a daily act of Christian worship', the key part of which had to 'operate around a Bible reading and its application to students' experience'. Sex education would be 'presented within a Christian moral framework, whereby self-respect and respect for others are seen in chastity outside of marriage and fidelity within it.'

If Thorne had seemed to be haplessly bounced into the plans for a Vardy Academy, the proposal that the Foundation should be handed a second Doncaster school, announced in the spring of 2004, had proven to be slightly more controversial. Though a spate of coverage of the Thorne scheme had failed to unite its opponents into any kind of organised force, it at least served to furnish the residents of Conisbrough and Denaby with information about what was planned for them. They were also blessed by the presence of the kind of people who would combine their disquiet with a tough resolve to contest the council's plans, both among teachers, and – perhaps more importantly – local parents.

Within a couple of days of the news that the council was considering the closure of Northcliffe comprehensive and the opening of another Vardy Academy, Kay Wilkinson and Tracy Morton had amassed a bulging file of information, and resolved to form CADPAG, the Conisbrough and Denaby Parents' Action Group. Their Labour councillors refused to discuss the matter until after June 2004's council elections, which left two months of what they called 'political purdah'; when they broke their silence, they were either noncommittal or brazenly enthusiastic about the Vardy proposal. The Liberal Democrats offered them their support in the run-up to 2004's local elections, but then quickly backed off, limply claiming that it would be best if the campaign wasn't compromised by politics ('It was as if somebody somewhere had said to them, "Don't get involved"') . Kay and Tracy also left a run of messages with their Labour MP, the Home Office Minister Caroline Flint. None were returned, until one of her assistants belatedly got in touch with Tracy and Kay after Flint's office had been contacted by *Newsnight*.

By the start of July, CADPAG had gathered close to 1,000 signatures on an anti-Vardy petition, and there had been three consultation meetings, one for parents with children at Northcliffe, and two for the general public. As far as the gauging of opinion went, they did not seem to offer very much: no option other than the Vardy proposal – such as a strategy for keeping

Northcliffe open and getting it out of Special Measures – was up for discussion, and the meetings followed a strict pattern: inquiries from the floor received a single answer from an assembled panel, with no comeback to the questioner. At the parents' meeting, attendance was rather compromised by the fact that the event had been scheduled for the same night as England's Euro 2004 match against Croatia.

'There was a line of men in suits,' said Tracy. 'John Burn, the educational adviser for the Vardy Foundation was there. David Vardy, Peter Vardy's brother, came to the parents' one. There were representatives of the City Academies programme from the DfES, various lawyers, and Mark Eales, the Doncaster director of education. And our local councillors would sit at the back, saying very little indeed.'

'If you asked a question, even if the panel said, "I don't know", you weren't allowed to make another point,' said Kay. 'It didn't seem like much of a consultation.'

'There *wasn't* any consulting,' said Tracy. 'Nobody asked *us* anything: "What do you think of this? What would your preferred options be?" We were not consulted.'

When parents asked John Burn about creationism, he feigned bafflement ('He just said, "I don't know what you mean by creationism." He asked *us* what it was'). At the parents' consultation meeting, Tracy quoted a speech Burn had given in which he had expressed the view that teachers at Vardy Schools should be 'full-time Christian workers'; he told her that it was a personal view not necessarily reflected in their plans for Conisbrough and Denaby. Perhaps most remarkably of all, though the Vardy Foundation had made much of their altruistic wish to assist an allegedly 'deprived' community, at least one of their pronouncements suggested a blithe insensitivity to any local hardship. 'At the first parents' meeting,' Kay recalled, 'Somebody asked David Vardy why they were only contributing two million while the government put in so much more. And he said, "Well, I can always take my money elsewhere. I can go and buy myself a yacht."'

As I later discovered when I met one of Northcliffe's teachers (who, given their uneasiness about the Council's dim view of the protests, spoke off the record), Northcliffe's staff had approached their consultations with both factual ammunition and a clever method at getting round the insistence that they were allowed one question each, and no comeback. Chains of questions were shared among teachers, so as to ensure that points could be pursued – as when one member of staff asked about the Vardy Foundation's stance on gay teachers.

'John Burn began his answer by saying, "Well, we think it's a sin,"' the teacher told me. 'When the staff gasped, he tried to broaden his response, by saying that they believed in including everyone, and they had people working in their schools of the Christian faith, other faiths, and no faith – no one would be excluded on the grounds of faith. That missed the point, really. The question wasn't *about* faith. And then the guy who had asked it was cut off by the chair of the meeting: a local councillor who was trying to enforce this one person, one question rule.

'But we had follow-up questions to that, distributed around the staff. They were along the lines of, "You seem to have made up your minds about which staff members are sinful and which aren't. How far does that extend? We have Muslim teachers on our staff. What about them?" John Burn said, "I don't think that's something we need to discuss at this point." He fudged it.'

If such meetings suggested that the proposed 'consultation' didn't amount to much at all, further developments only seemed to confirm it. At first, Doncaster's Education Authorities talked about rejecting the Vardy proposal if a majority of local opinion was against it. As the summer of 2004 progressed, that was changed to a 'sizeable majority'. Lest anyone think that they were planning some rigorous, verifiable gauging of local opinion, however, their next move suggested either chronic ineptitude or an absurd kind of cynicism. In July, Doncaster's Executive Director of Education and Culture sent households in Conisbrough and Denaby a similar wonkily-photocopied form to the one had been circulated in Thorne. As had happened up the road, it remained unclear how many of them had been sent out, or what importance they were accorded.

In the meantime, Tracy, Kay and the Conisbrough and Denaby Parents' Action Group were anxiously waiting. They had extracted the odd concession from the Vardy Foundation – most notably, a guarantee that all pupils on roll at Northcliffe, along with those Year 6 primary pupils scheduled to go there in 2005, would be admitted to the proposed Academy – but that left the prospects of younger local children open to doubt. On account of their supposed reputation for soaring academic excellence, Academies tend to attract a volume of applications out of all proportion to available places: at the Vardy Foundation's King's Academy, for example, the ratio hovers at around 2 to 1. In Conisbrough and Denaby, what would happen to the kids who were either rejected or not entered at all? The Academies generation was rearing up to be the first for over half a century whose life chances were so pegged to a mixture of informational wherewithal and parental pushiness.

For all their resolve, I wondered how Kay and Tracy viewed the seemingly likely prospect of Northcliffe's closure, and their kids' induction into the world of the Vardy Foundation. 'That is very frightening,' said Tracy. 'I can't even think about it. I can't bear the thought of my daughter sitting in the classroom being taught by someone who's trying to lace her education with these extreme kind of Christian ideologies. It horrifies me.'

As 2004 rolled on, I kept in touch with Tracy and Kay. They initially expected an announcement in July; as it turned out, the council's decision about their plans for Conisbrough and Denaby were postponed three times, and finally scheduled for early November. The results of the consultation would be published five days before the announcement; a ruse, it appeared, to minimise the chance of any disputes abouts its reliability gaining momentum. Along the way, council spokespeople told the local press that local people were 60 per cent in favour of the Vardy Plan, a claim that came with no factual back-up, but convinced the Parents' Action Group that bad news was pretty much inevitable.

On Wednesday October 13, however, Doncaster's mayor served notice that Northcliffe Comprehensive would remain open, and the Vardy plan was thereby binned. 'A significant number of the local community, the teachers and the pupils have spoken loud and clear,' went Martin Winter's statement. 'They do not want it for their children.' By way of betraying his annoyance, the mayor duly appeared on the BBC's *Look North* programme, making the nebulous claim that, as against the educational miracles promised by the Academy plan, four out of five Northcliffe pupils currently 'failed' – exactly what they failed *at* remained a mystery. Sir Peter Vardy, meanwhile, haughtily offered the opinion that 'far from celebrating, [the Parents' Action Group] should be reflecting on the opportunity they have denied their children for an education of the very highest standard in state-of-the-art facilities.'

A few days after the announcement, I went back to Conisbrough. Tracy and Kay were at work in the Windmill Centre; the pensioners were in the midst of another game of bingo. Under a nearby desk was a wadge of copies of the Doncaster *Free Press*, whose front pages featured the headline 'Academy Plan Axed'. There was a palpable atmosphere of relief and vindication, though CADPAG had a new fight on their hands: pressuring the council to belatedly release the results of the Conisborough and Denaby consultation, so that it might be used to help other anti-Academy campaigners. As far as the activities of the Vardy Foundation are concerned, CADPAG's assistance may soon be required: chillingly, Sir Peter Vardy has talked about his schools eventually seeing to the education of 10,000 pupils.

'I believe that when the Vardy Foundation came in, they were given Thorne and Conisbrough as a done deal,' said Kay. 'And when we sprouted up and made all the noise we possibly could, I think they realised it wasn't going to be as big a walkover as they'd expected.'

'We know that the mayor's very, very cross,' said Tracy. 'All he can actually be seen to do is to support Northcliffe from this point on. They can't close it, because they couldn't find places for the kids. Realistically, they have to support the school and get it out of Special Measures.'

While I was there, I also decided to spend some time in Thorne. There were eleven months left until the opening of the

Vardy Academy, but no shortage of news about developments. The entire contents of Thorne Grammar's library was reportedly being handed back to the council, because the Vardy Foundation had decided that each and every book was 'no longer appropriate'. Though the Foundation had made much of its alleged concern for the school's surrounding community, a council youth centre on the school site was being turfed off. New premises had been found, but they would not be available until nine months after the Academy opened; as a result, Thorne's youth workers were worried about losing touch with the young people they were meant to help. To cap it all, flats were going to be built and sold on the school site, though no one seemed very sure about what would happen to the proceeds.

Within the school, meanwhile, the transition from comprehensive to Academy was proceeding at speed. According to the teacher I met, he and his colleagues were in the midst of interviews – 'encounters', in Vardy-speak – with their new employers, and some of the most telling exchanges had focused on the criteria by which staff selected texts appropriate for their lessons. 'It got fairly direct,' he told me. 'They said, "What books would you teach?" I said, "Whatever books are on the syllabus." But that evidently wasn't what they wanted. With another teacher, they asked the same question, and it became clear that they were steering the conversation towards something biblical.'

There was also the small matter of the Vardy Foundation's record on exclusions. Schools run by LEAs suffer financial penalties for every pupil they expel; Academies are liberated from such rules. Thus, in its first year, the Vardy school in Middlesbrough had excluded twenty-seven pupils – ten times the national average. Staffroom opinion in Thorne suggested that if a similar purge came to pass at the new Academy, some of the town's more difficult kids would end up at the nearby comprehensive in Hatfield. The Vardy Foundation would doubtless crow about improved exam results; schools left within the control of Doncaster's LEA would bear the burden they had so conveniently sloughed off.

That afternoon, I decided to sample some local opinion. My first stop-off was at a local estate agents, where the two women I met seemed only too enthusiastic about the opening of the Academy. Katie, a former Thorne Grammar pupil, said that the town had welcomed the Vardy Foundation 'with open arms', thanks to both their promise of new buildings and facilities, and their avowed aim of enforcing stringent standards of discipline. The latter point was echoed by other people I met: with such concerns in mind, the Vardy Foundation had already circulated the Academy's disciplinary code, set out over two columns devoted to 'acts' and their various punishments. Fighting would bring 'suspension and consideration of merits'; the apparently graver sin of smoking was to be met with a 'suspension and final warning'.

Some of the Academy's effects on the town were already becoming clear. 'It's doing wonders for house sales, I tell you that,' said Katie. She and her colleague Judy could only think of one group of locals who were expressing any opposition: the residents of a street called Church Walk, angry about the noise made by the construction of new school buildings.

But what, I wondered, about the most worrying aspect of the Vardy scheme: the malign bundle of ideas they disingenuously termed a 'Christian ethos'? 'I was taught like that: saying the

Lord's Prayer and all that,' said Judy, who was hoping to get her son a place at the Academy. 'It doesn't do anyone any harm.'

It went a bit further than that, though, I said. The Vardy Foundation thought that creationism and evolution were competing 'faith positions'. They'd come to the conclusion that Harry Potter books amounted to works of the occult. Judy let out a fatalistic chuckle. 'I don't think many people are that clued up about the religious side of it all. I was quite happy about my son going there till you told me that.'

Naturally, none of the sumptuous Vardy Foundation literature that she had received made mention of such matters. Their latest newsletter brought news of fresh new appointments, the necessity of applying for places at least a year early, and 'outstanding' GCSE achievements at their two existing schools. There was also a 24-page prospectus featuring a watercolour of the Academy, replete with gleaming new buildings and what looked like its own lake, and promises of 'raising standards and creating opportunities for the children of our area'.

On the back was a photograph of Mr Blair, his hands outstretched in the vicar-ish pose that he habitually uses to convey passionate belief. Next to it was a seven-line quote from March 2004, in which the Prime Minister enthused about the Vardy Foundation's school in Middlesbrough. It amounted, he said, to 'one of the best examples of modern social justice that I can think of'.

5 The Great Beyond

As far as eight million residents of the UK are concerned, such New Labour inventions as Academies, outsourced LEAs and Foundation Hospitals have yet to arrive. Thanks to Scottish and Welsh devolution, arguably the most spectacular of the policies enacted in the Blair government's first term, politics in those two countries is altogether different from the current Westminster model: the key opposition parties sit to the left of the Labour Party, and political realities are not quite as bleak as the ones that prevail in England. 'Socialism is alive and well in Scotland and Wales,' Roy Hattersley told me. I'm not sure I'd go quite that far, but I can see his point.

In Westminster, Mr Blair can be assured that, no matter how alarming his reform ideas may appear, he is gifted with both that sky-high majority and the tendency of Tory opposition to crash-land to his right, thus ensuring that (1) New Labour looks like the lesser of two quasi-Thatcherite evils, and (2) any challenge to the basis of Mr Blair's ideas ('choice', usually) is kept on the margins. In Cardiff and Edinburgh politics, however, are rather different – and given that health and education are among the responsibilities handed over to the Scottish Parliament and Welsh Assembly, even the most zealous Blairites have to tread a little more carefully.

In Scotland, both Labour terms have found them in coalition with the Liberal Democrats – whose most famous political victories have seen the blunting of Labour's tuition fees proposals, and the introduction of free long-term care for the elderly. In Wales, the ruling Labour administration (whose first term also saw an alliance with the Lib Dems) is headed by Rhodri Morgan, fond of characterising himself as a representative of 'classic Labour', and curtly dismissive of some of the government's more market-embracing ideas. Equally importantly, in both countries, the opposition provided by the countries' nationalists (along with the more marginal Greens and, north of the border, the proudly revolutionary Scottish Socialists) decisively tilts arguments leftwards – for aside from their beliefs in independence, the Scottish National Party and Plaid Cymru hold fast to some heartwarmingly old-fashioned notions: not least, the idea that private interests tend to be ill-suited to the provision of public services.

Their campaign literature often reads like something not only from another political age, but focused on a very different world to the comfortable, consumerist place recurrently mapped out by New Labour. 'Britain today stands out as one of the most unequal countries in Europe, and this inequality is evident both socially and geographically,' ran Plaid's 2001 General Election manifesto. 'There is a huge gap between regions and social classes, with serious problems of exclusion.' Of late, the SNP's rhetoric has not been nearly so strident, but it has still alighted on themes missing from English debate: most notably, the crushing economic hegemony of the South East of England. The effects of all this on the wider political scene are clear: rather than faux-debates about choice, or 'Localism', or the so-called personalisation of public services, at least some of Scottish and Welsh politics is still bound up with such matters as the distribution of wealth and power – what used to be called the fundamentals.

This is not quite to suggest that any frustrated English progressive should make for the borders and prepare for life in a place where politics actually works. In Scotland in particular, devolution is often held to have encouraged the worst aspects of modern government: not least the kind of reckless profligacy that has seen the cost of the Holyrood Parliament building rise from £40 million to £400 million. Moreover, any Labour Party supporter who clings to the idea that things in Scotland and Wales might form the basis for some imagined re-balancing of the party's thinking would do well to look at the odd recent development. Despite robust opposition, both countries have embraced PFI. There are also clear signs that the English party's tolerance of the road taken in Edinburgh and Cardiff is running out: in Wales, alleged healthcare failures have seen loud claims that Rhodri Morgan should embrace the government line on the NHS; last summer saw a Scottish Labour policy forum being asked – in the words of one newspaper report – 'what Scotland can learn from Tony Blair's controversial Foundation Hospitals experiment'.

For the time being, however, what has happened outside England poses some compelling questions. The most pertinent to this book is simple: given their role in pulling the political agenda away from New Labour, along with the admirable Westminster voting records of their handful of MPs, should those who are worried about the idea of another New Labour term think about supporting the nationalists?

The SNP

' I dislike this Prime Minister even more than I disliked
Margaret Thatcher.'

2003 was a bad year for both nationalist parties. In the elections for the Scottish Parliament and Welsh Assembly, their share of the vote tumbled and set in chain a predictable set of consequences: claims that devolution had rather squashed the desire for independence on which Plaid Cymru and the SNP depended, and bouts of internal debate that saw the resignations of both their leaders. Having initially gone for the Peter Mandelson option and claimed he was a fighter not a quitter, Plaid's Ieuan Wyn Jones resigned that May (confusingly, four months later he made a comeback as Plaid leader in the Welsh Assembly). The SNP's John Swinney hung on a little longer, but after disappointing results in last year's Euro elections, he too decided to go.

As I discovered in the course of my research, Swinney's time as SNP leader had not been the most inspiring period in the party's history. Bespectacled, studious and off-puttingly dour, he often seemed to be pushing them on to the same washed-out place as the Liberal Democrats – emphasising their business credentials, pledging to cut corporation tax, and placing such an accent on managerial respectability that even the party's commitment to independence had been underplayed.

All that formed the backdrop to my meeting one July afternoon with Alex Salmond, the SNP's leader between 1990 and 2000, who had since left his seat in the Scottish Parliament and concentrated on commanding the party's five MPs in the House of Commons. Having played a pivotal role in pushing the SNP towards a left-of-centre, social democratic approach, his time in charge of the party had seen its decisive arrival in the political mainstream; these days, he seemed content with life as the SNP's one true elder statesman. As if to underwrite his seniority, at one point a young and strangely silent underling arrived with two cigarettes and promptly disappeared. 'I've given up,' Mr Salmond assured me. 'I *have*. I'm just having the odd relapse.' He self-consciously slapped his stomach. 'But I put on two stone.'

Though his time since stepping down as leader might have suggested some kind of dotage, Mr Salmond's work in Parliament has often been inspirational: on Iraq in particular, he has been everything that Charles Kennedy has not – sharp, forensic, outspoken, and willing to place the war in the context of America's need for oil. When we met, it was surely some token of the esteem in which he was held that he was already being encouraged to return to his old job. Unfortunately, he claimed to be unmoved. 'I had a great time leading the SNP, a really fantastic time,' he said. 'But ten years is a long time. Blair's been Prime Minister seven years, and he looks like death warmed up. I'm not moaning about it – that's the job and I loved doing it. But that was then, and now's now.'

Instead, he betrayed an alpha-male kind of regality, surveying the field of leadership candidates in the manner of a cool-headed kingmaker. Thus far, three people had decided to stand: Roseanna Cunningham (deputy leader, aimed to be 'more clearly left of centre'), Nicola Sturgeon (justice spokeswoman, favoured 'more youthful energy and a clearer sense of direction') and Mike Russell (who promised 'a radical plan for party renewal'). He claimed to rate them all, though he strayed close to issuing damningly faint praise. 'Roseanna,' he said, 'is some-one I've known for a large number of years – someone who won in rural Perthshire as a republican. So whatever else you might say about her, she's no feart [not easily scared]. Nicola is, by a long way, the most talented young person in Scottish politics. She's thirty-three. She's got a huge amount of talent; she's got to develop other skills, but she's got every political gift. And Michael – well, Michael's a great force. A great friend of mine. He's the outsider, obviously. A big intellectual. An interesting guy.' He paused for a moment. 'English,' he said, quietly. 'Or English-born, anyway.'

Whoever won, Mr Salmond claimed to be certain of where the SNP was now duty-bound to travel: away from Mr Swinney's charisma-free respectability ('He was compared with the local bank manager – but you could be a lot worse: you could be the local crook') towards a re-emphasis on Scottish independence, along with more vociferous opposition to New Labour. On the latter score, even under their recent washed-out leadership, he claimed their credentials had long been in place: instead of PFI, for example, the SNP advocated a system of publicly owned trusts which could borrow money for hospitals and schools at public sector rates of interest and thereby nullify some of that policy's worst aspects. When it came to income tax, though their current policy of charging a rate of 45 per cent on earnings over £100,000 actually put them to the right of the Lib Dems, he claimed this amounted to a mere detail.

'Well, yeah,' he said, slightly hesitantly. 'Except . . . Well, I mean . . . As I remember, with our last manifesto, there was a bit more to it than that. There was a progressive National Insurance ceil-ing, which would have had a major impact on redistribution.'

He exhaled slowly, and managed to regain his thread. 'The SNP is to the left of New Labour,' he assured me. 'We believe in redistribution, we believe in public purpose, we don't believe in services being dominated or provided by private capital, we believe public services should be run in the public interest – or as we say in Scotland, for the common weal. In Scotland, that's a very strong and resonant philosophy, which stretches back a long way, and means – well, look at the things that are really important in Scotland, that stem from a Scottish view of the world. Like education: if you look back, the first Scottish public legislation was the provision of education in every parish. The first public legislation in England was the Poor Law.'

So much for history. On the subject of political geography, I wondered whether there was something unavoidably strange about sitting in SW1 talking about the SNP's next pitch for seats in the Commons. With health, education, justice, housing, policing and God knows what else all debated and decided in Edinburgh, what political terrain was left for the next Westminster election?

'I think the SNP have to be very clear about this,' he said. 'Traditionally, obviously, a Westminster election was the main election. Now, we have to forget any notion of that – the idea that you're going to win independence by fluking a majority of Scottish seats. That option – and it was never a real option – is clearly not the main theatre where this battle will be fought. This battle's going to be fought in Scottish elections, in a Scottish context.'

Nonetheless, he said, the lines of debate at the next General Election would be clear enough. First, though the seats in which the SNP might conceivably worry the Labour Party were few (give or take Scotland's looming boundary changes there are four, in fact: Dundee East, Aberdeen North, Inverness East and the Western Isles), it was worth voting for them simply on the basis of keeping the Westminster government fearful of further SNP advances and thereby alert to both Scottish interests and the kind of policies the party put forward. In addition, there was the small matter of Iraq. 'I suppose we'd also be saying things like, "If you want MPs who'd be guaranteed to vote against Blair's military adventures, wherever they might be in the future, then you've got a safe bet with SNP MPs."'

At the time of the war, John Swinney had been in charge of the SNP, and plagued by stories about an alleged 'wobble' when it came to the party's opposition. This, Mr Salmond claimed, was nonsense: there had been brief uncertainty, but it was caused by the prospect of an invasion backed by the UN. Once that fairly illusory possibility had vanished, the SNP's position was hardly in doubt. 'In one speech I suggested the Prime Minister was on his way to hell,' he said, sounding slightly surprised at himself. 'I said he'd answer to a higher court than the House of Commons. And I don't wear my religion on my sleeve like the Prime Minister occasionally does. I don't buy, "Everybody knew or thought there were weapons, or the risk of weapons." I believe Blair has never believed there were weapons of mass destruction. I believe the country was taken to war on a deliberate lie, for other reasons. And I believe he'll have to account for that.'

'Blair has a character defect,' he concluded, 'which makes him look for the crunch occasion. He wants the adrenaline fix. He needed to go to the wire on tuition fees, even when he didn't have to. He needed to go to the wire on Foundation Hospitals. He needs the great crusade, the last battle: he needs to be at the centre of events, where he's risking all – one crusader on his horse, charging into the enemy. He's never happier than when he's doing that. But when he does that, he gambles with other people's chips, and the other people count the cost of what he's done. And that's why I dislike this Prime Minister even more than I disliked Margaret Thatcher.'

I came away from my time with Mr Salmond feeling something that my encounters with politicians had usually failed to produce: admiration, tempered a little by a suspicion that the SNP was not quite the leftist force he made out, but there all the same. At least a quarter of my tape was given over to that increasingly rare pastime: the discussion of ideas. I liked the fact that, at least fifteen minutes after I had packed my belongings away and said goodbye, he had followed me to the lift, still frantically talking – this time about the fact that, in the event of a hung parliament and the replacement of Blair by Brown, the SNP would be all but guaranteed to support the formation of a Labour government. Moreover, if so many of my encounters with politicians had found me confronting people who perhaps knew they could not take the radical step of speaking their minds, Mr Salmond seemed equipped with that rare political virtue: something close to sincerity.

Some time later came news that slightly undermined all that, though it was hardly much of a surprise. Roseanna, Mike and Nicola were now apparently doomed; three weeks into the SNP's leadership campaign, Alex Salmond had decided to stand again for his old job. There was little doubt that he would soar to victory.

Plaid Cymru

'One vote doesn't make a difference, but a thousand votes can.'

'All we've got in Parliament in at the moment, between Labour and the Tories, is a managerial argument. The Tories say, "We'll give you absolute choice" and Labour say, "We'll give you a bit of choice." What the *hell* is that about? Nobody's asking the basic question: What choice do you have on a sink estate when your children have to go to a school down the road because you can't get them in any other school? Everything the main parties are doing is pushing towards a society in which the aspiration will be, in old-fashioned terms, to be middle class, but you'll have an increasingly large underclass. You're not supposed to use that word any more, but what do you call people who don't vote, can't take part in choice, have a minimum wage at the very most? That's a society which will have become corrupted.'

Those words were spoken – in more soft-spoken tones than they suggest – by Simon Thomas, the Plaid Cymru MP for the far-west constituency of Ceredigion. I had arranged to meet him after seeing him on an edition of *Question Time* for which he had taken his seat among motley company indeed: Norman Tebbit, Baroness Amos (Leader of the House of Lords and the first black woman to sit in the British cabinet), Sheikh Hamza Yusuf (a high-profile American Muslim convert-turned-cleric) and Rhona 'I'm a Celebrity' Cameron, whose embarrassingly threadbare contributions were crystallised by the bizarre admission that she wasn't really 'a political person'.

Despite looking distinctly bemused, Simon – the first male Westminster MP to wear an earring, which surely allows for the use of his Christian name – was an unexpected delight: on most of the subjects thrown at the panel, I found myself agreeing with just about everything he said. The prospect of spending an hour or two with an MP and not coming away with chewed knuckles and dashed hopes was enough to prompt a call to his Westminster office, and the arranging of lunch in the tourist-sprinkled town of Cardigan, where he ordered a goat's cheese salad (in Welsh, naturally), and managed to impress me yet again, talking volubly about the kind of politics that grips millions of minds across the industrial world, but can never seem to find its way into the Commons. The allegedly groovy Lembit Öpik had expressed apologetic ignorance when I mentioned Naomi Klein's *No Logo*; Simon was intimately acquainted with that book, regularly in email contact with the anti-globalisation godhead George Monbiot, and happy to use a vocabulary sprinkled with such Westminster taboos as environmental sustainability and corporate power.

Even when it came to Welsh independence, an issue that can leave plenty of people – including me – either indifferent or harbouring predictable lefty-liberal worries about the dangers of vehement nationalism, he had an argument that came out sounding unexpectedly seductive. 'In a modern, post-industrial world, it's the smaller states that succeed in maintaining social cohesion, and sharing wealth; and it's the larger, more centralised states that are starting to fail,' he said. 'Take the United States: you can be wonderfully successful in terms of your GDP and all the rest of it, but if 40 per cent of your people are living on the breadline, that's not any kind of success.'

The same analysis, he said, comfortably fitted the UK, where the overweening importance attached to voters in Basildon, Chingford and Chelmsford had long made the woes of

Pontypridd and Bradford and Paisley something of an irrelevance. 'We're the most unequal state in the European Union,' he said. 'Some people argue that Greece is a bit more unequal, but there you're talking about things like a comparison between Athens and the Greek islands. In terms of large unitary states, we're definitely the most unequal, the most polarised. But in smaller states, I think different things become possible. One is that you can build in more of a sense of national journey, a national purpose. I don't think there's a national purpose shared across the UK. That's been a big part of Plaid's work over the last ten years: the idea that political aims are things that you come up with together and you can work towards. Some people would call that nationalism. At the heart of it, I have an emotional nationalism somewhere, but you also try and make sure that what you're thinking makes sense.'

Of course, not all of Plaid Cymru's membership are quite so politically perfect. Some – like Seimon Glyn, a Gwynedd councillor who mucked up the party's pitch for the 2001 General Election – have seemed happy to let their emotional nationalism rise to the surface: on a radio phone-in a few months prior to the campaign, Mr Glyn, getting rather overheated about migration to rural Wales from England, suggested that the numbers of émigrés from across the border should be monitored, and that those who made the move ought to take compulsory Welsh lessons. As is apparently all but traditional, the pro-Labour Welsh edition of the *Daily Mirror* splurged out a brief run of outraged headlines about a supposed 'race row' ('Voice of hate: "Racist" Plaid Councillor's attack on the English'), before the Plaid leadership attempted to assure English-speaking floating voters that Mr Glyn was only speaking for himself and hoof him back to the party's fringes.

'I just felt that was a reflection of the nature of the press and the politics we're in,' said Simon. 'What he said was plainly a bit nuts – but all political parties have nuts like that in them. The Labour Party seized it as a huge opportunity to portray us as racist – *all* of us – and the press played along with it. There's an issue at the heart of what he was trying to address – a housing crisis, and rising house prices – but he was blaming the people who are riding the market for the political problems of what the government are doing, or the way the market has gone.' (By way of proving that Plaid is a slightly more enlightened organisation than its enemies are wont to suggest, last year's Euro elections saw the election of three Plaid Cymru councillors drawn from South Wales's Muslim communities.)

The convenient caricature of Plaid as the political wing of an arcane, embittered cult fixated on little more than holiday cottages and bilingual road signs doesn't really stand up. In addition to promises relating to increased powers for the Welsh Assembly, its 2001 manifesto pledges included commitments to suspend PFI, increase the minimum wage, reduce the power of Britain's supermarkets and introduce taxes on corporate polluters. To a far greater extent than the Scottish National Party, their pronouncements are shot through with an opposition to New Labour founded on principle – even, to use a very incongruous word, *ideology*. Better still, their place outside Westminster's more charmed circles leaves them free to indulge in the odd burst of inspired political creativity – as in August 2004, when the news-grabbing attempt to heal the democratic wounds caused by the Iraq war by subjecting Mr Blair to the long-forgotten process of parliamentary impeachment was led by the Plaid MP Adam Price. It may have been a knowing stunt, but it was surely the kind of tactic from which those opposed to New Labour would do well to learn.

When it came to Plaid's appeal to dismayed Labour voters at the next election, Simon Thomas laid out an argument based on two foundations, both of which might serve to offset either unease about Plaid's Welsh-language zealots, or any misgivings about the far-off prospect of Welsh independence. First, he said, the merest glance at the voting record of the party's pocket-sized group in the Commons suggested that having a Plaid MP amounted to much the same thing as being represented by a left-wing Labour maverick. In addition, there was the effect that an increased Plaid vote at the next General Election might have on politics in Wales: with Labour's Welsh MPs seemingly trying their best to elbow Rhodri Morgan away from the 'classic Labour' agenda ('which is a horribly undemocratic way to behave,' said Simon), weakening their clout might prove to be a good way of maintaining the Welsh Assembly's political independence.

Either way, it was transparently obvious where his party was coming from. 'If you want to register a protest, if you want to have even the inkling of change,' he said, between his last mouthfuls of goat's cheese, 'then Plaid is the only real option. The Lib Dems are not seriously challenging the Labour Party from the left, from the perspective of actually challenging the institutional set-up that's creating the society we've got now. One vote doesn't make a difference, but a thousand votes can.'

If Simon largely managed to sound both optimistic and ever-so-slightly visionary, his parting thoughts were more downbeat. Plaid, he said, had long found difficulty pushing its way into a political debate that, for all Wales's political differences, was still stitched into much the same limitations that so bedevil Westminster. 'It's not just the political culture that rules things out,' he said, 'it's the media culture as well. You can't discuss a lot of issues, because the press and the broadcasters just aren't interested in them. It's, "*This* isn't the argument."'

As British politics was thereby hacked down to the most yawn-inducing essence, a small party like Plaid found itself compromised by what Simon called 'the lack of a decent left-wing discourse'. Compounding such frustrations was the fact that, thanks to Wales's Labour-dominated map, in addition to its four Westminster MPs the party had a realistic possibility of securing just one more – in Ynys Mon, the North Welsh constituency represented by a commendably rebellious Labour backbencher named Albert Owen.

For millions of those who might be charmed by Plaid Cymru's hostility to New Labour, there is – of course – an additional sticking point. For most people, they are not an option which actually exists.

The Green Party

'Money cannot be eaten.'

In which case, there's always the Greens: that higgledy-piggledy political force who will not elect a single leader or nail down their policy stances in much fewer than 5,000 words at a time (for details, visit the requisite section of www.greenparty. org.uk), but who seem to be slowly in the ascendant. New Labour's hesitant embrace of proportional representation has been the key, giving the Greens toe-holds in the Scottish Parliament, Welsh Assembly and Greater London Authority, as well as allowing two Green MEPs to carve out a working life in Brussels. If the achievements seem modest, they actually represent a heartening success story; less than ten years ago, the party's membership had dropped to around 3,000. In the proud words of Darren Johnson, one of two Green members of the GLA and the party's candidate for London Mayor in 2000 and 2004, 'The Green Party is now a much stronger force in British politics. We have a much higher profile. We have many more members, and more elected Greens than ever before.'

I met Darren – again, he may deserve a 'Mr', but he's under forty and he was wearing jeans – in the Green Party compound at City Hall, the buffed-up glass construction that sits across the river from the Tower of London. The GLA was in recess: he had come in for the afternoon to begin his preparation for its recall in September, and spend an hour answering my questions. For all his eagerness, Darren took a bit of warming up, spending the first twenty minutes of our meeting burdened by lengthy *um*-ing and *ah*-ing and betraying a dispiriting reliance on such verbal tics as 'stuff like that'. Worse still, he initially seemed to be suffering from a touch of political fuzziness, sounding not unlike a left-wing version of one of the more confused senior members of the Lib Dems.

He had joined the Greens in the mid-80s as a twenty year-old resident of Preston, fired up by all manner of issues but unable to find a home in what passed for orthodox party politics. It was probably some token of his uncompromising outlook that, though many of us had been happy to stand by Neil Kinnock, Darren viewed him as a kind of proto-Blairist sell-out. 'Already by then, you'd started to see him backtrack on the nuclear agenda and stuff like that,' he explained. 'And I mean . . . Things that were really doing it for me at the time were the lesbian and gay rights agenda, the environment post-Chernobyl, peace, animal issues – factory farming and that sort of stuff. I became a vegetarian about that time, I think . . . Definitely coming through the miners' strike and everything with a very, sort of, you know, left-of-centre perspective. But I saw it all as a rag-bag of single issues. Then I came across a copy of the Green Party's manifesto. I thought, "Oh wow – this wraps it all up together in a nice coherent philosophy."'

And what, I wondered, was the ideological glue that held it all together?

'Erm . . . I think it was just bringing together these strands into a green vision, rather than it being a sort of left-of-centre thing with add-ons, really. It was in terms of – well, the Green Party's always stood for environmental justice, social justice, peace, and, erm, participation.'

If that sounded rather vague, a subsequent trawl through the part of the Greens' website labelled 'Philosophical basis' offered only limited help. One passage (numbered 'PB101') was laid out as a poem: 'Only after the last tree has been cut down/ Only after the last river has been poisoned/ Only after the last fish has been caught/ Only then will you find that money cannot be eaten.' That's right.

In fairness, one need not puzzle over the party's textual mountains to divine where the Greens stand. They are – and this may be stating the obvious – squarely on the side of that nationwide constituency whose worldview is built on overarching alarm at the world's slide towards ecological collapse, a fate made all the more imminent by some of the aspects of modern living that the people resident in the political mainstream take for granted: reliance on the car, a belief that endless economic expansion is a given (among the most withering insults in the Green vocabulary is 'growthist'), an acceptance that, in the consumer sphere, nothing speaks as loudly as simple convenience. By way of an antidote, the Greens yield to a vision of an altogether gentler, more co-operative Britain in which polluters are decisively tamed, local communities turn their back on Asda and Tesco and work towards a new self-sufficiency, and there is no shame in getting the bus.

Lurking within all that, thankfully, are the kind of hardened policy commitments that electoral politics demands: a belief in returning the railways to public ownership, opposition to the expansion of the UK's airports and motorways, hostility to New Labour's privatisation programmes, and – but of course – a proposed ban on GM foods, along with an end to factory farming and the export of live animals. There is also a commendably robust attachment to some of the ideas that attracted hundreds of thousands of people during the 1980s, only to fade from view: the Greens advocate unilateral nuclear disarmament, British withdrawal from Nato, and the UK allying itself with the world's non-aligned countries.

If all that sounded quite appealing, I wondered whether there were items within the Greens' policy portfolio that served to confirm more malign views of their beliefs. For example, I had recently come across a report in the *Guardian* alleging that they 'want a 20 m.p.h. limit imposed on all but major roads'. That slightly bothered me, I said – having begun my journey to London by spending forty minutes travelling along the A438 to Hereford station, I had wondered whether the Greens might force me to pack sandwiches and take a couple of hours.

'Well no,' said Darren. 'It's a policy for roads in residential areas. It means going from thirty to twenty.'

So, I said, trying not to sound like an outraged spokesman for the RAC, roads that currently had a speed limit of 60 m.p.h. would be left alone?

'Yeah. Or they might be fifty, or whatever. We're not talking about a blanket measure. What we're talking about is reducing the thirty miles an hour speed limit to twenty, because all the statistics have shown that you've got a much greater chance of surviving an accident at that speed. It's all about creating a safer street environment, so more people can walk and cycle.'

I also wondered about their commitment, built into Darren's recent campaign for the mayoralty, to extend congestion charging to the whole of London. As a one-time resident of W12, I had seen the unquestionable benefits of the scheme – what concerned me was whether it was fair to levy a fee on someone journeying from, say, Southend to Ilford to visit their grandmother.

Darren looked mildly apologetic. 'I mean . . . I think, with hindsight . . . Well, this did go down particularly badly with certain sections of the electorate. I think, you know, we could have looked at taking up that policy in a different way, either promoting it through a national road-pricing scheme, or a smaller congestion-charging zone. I'd be happy to throw my hands up and say that that needs looking at again. I can't say fairer than that, can I?'

Such was one of the little luxuries of life on the edge of the political map. Given the Greens' distance from political power, Darren seemed unabashed about the fact that large swathes of their policies – on taxation, for example – amounted to work in progress. And in some places, it was hardly doing them much harm: recent weeks had seen a burst of reports about the dizzying possibility of the Greens winning their first parliamentary seat in the Brighton Pavilion constituency, where the election of six Green councillors at the 2004 local elections and a commendable share of the votes for the European Parliament had seen them push the Labour Party into third place. Labour had reacted by issuing predictable warnings about a massed defection to the Greens causing an unforeseen victory for the Tories, but in the Greens' equally inevitable view, the alarm was misplaced: even if the Labour vote came crashing down, a Tory victory would require a larger share than the 25.1 per cent they managed in 2001 – and central Brighton was not the kind of place where many people would be suddenly flocking to Michael Howard.

'What I've found is that the biggest barrier to people voting Green isn't our image, or sections of our policies,' said Darren. 'It's about whether we can win or not. If we can convince a critical mass that we actually can, which has happened in other places . . . Certainly in Brighton, I think we're reaching that position. And I think there are other seats where we can do exceptionally well. I'll be standing in Lewisham and Deptford at the next election – and even though winning it is a long shot, I reckon we can get a decent second place there, and win the seat the time after.'

There was but one shadow in the midst of the Greens' gleaming new dawn. In the build-up to 2004's European and local elections, a nuisance had materialised: the Respect Coalition, that uneasy alliance of the Socialist Workers Party, the Muslim Association of Britain and George Galloway MP, pledged to succeed where countless radical *groupuscules* had failed and mount a potent left-wing challenge to the Labour Party. There had been a flurry of speculation about Respect and the Greens forging an electoral arrangement, but any overtures had come to nothing. Ever since, Respect's leaders had been expressing their displeasure. 'I don't call them the Greens, I call them the Whites,' said the assuredly Caucasian Mr Galloway. 'If you look at their candidates, you see middle-class whites.'

Darren Johnson had always been resolutely against any accord. 'We're a party with a strong base of support who are on the up,' he told me, slightly testily. 'I didn't see why we should agree to stand down anywhere.'

It would surely form one of the tinier footnotes of British political history, but I was still curious: had there been some kind of abortive summit meeting?

'There was a *meal*,' said Darren. 'Some people met up. I was one of the people who was asked to go, but I thought it was pointless. We've got a strong identity – why would we want to form an alliance with a new party that no one's ever heard of? We'll see how long they last.'

The Respect Coalition

'As you probably know, I can shake hands with anybody.'

In his office at Portcullis House, George Galloway – the MP for Glasgow Kelvin, zealous anti-Blairist and self-styled friend of Fidel Castro – was sitting in close proximity to a couple of scented candles and a ring-binder emblazoned with the image of Che Guevara, and fleshing out the most recent episodes of his political life: his response to the Iraq war, his expulsion from the Labour Party and his new role as the figurehead of the Respect

Coalition. He also mentioned his doomed date with the Greens. 'I laid on a huge slap-up dinner for them,' he said, 'and before we finished the soup' – he emphasised the last word, as if to underline his sense of hurt – 'it became clear that there was no point in this dinner, because they were saying that under no circumstances could they stand down anywhere. So we would have to cease to exist, which isn't much of a basis for a negotiation.'

When we met, Respect were bravely preparing themselves for their first test, putting up a raft of candidates – including Mr Galloway – for 2004's Euro elections. Partly by way of assisting their campaign effort, Mr Galloway was also promoting *I'm Not the Only One*, a rhetorical political memoir that, perhaps like its author, was demonstrably sincere but occasionally prone to borderline ludicrousness. My favourite passage had been lodged in my mind for a couple of weeks: 'When I have addressed gatherings of people who see the world like me in Paris, Madrid, Amsterdam, Athens, even Managua, Hiroshima, Beijing, I have never felt I stood on foreign land. As I told my daughter Lucy many years ago, when she asked me if I was Scottish or British, "My flag is red, my country is the future."'

Though he occasionally affected his swashbuckling man-of-destiny schtick, Mr Galloway was not the demagogic left-wing Bond villain I'd been led to expect. It would be fair to say that we had a laugh, not least when I asked him about his new comrades the Socialist Workers Party, surely the kind of Trotskyist headbangers to whom his book referred as 'fanatics' and 'fantasists' (for all his radicalism, Mr Galloway claimed to have never been a pal of what he terms the 'ultra-left'). To compound the incongruity, Respect were also in talks with the Socialist Party, an all-but-irrelevant rump that represented the last traces of my old friends from Militant. I wondered if it felt strange, metaphorically shaking hands with people he had once apparently despised. 'Well, no,' he said, as a smile crept across his face. 'As you probably know, I can shake hands with anybody.'

This, of course, was a reference to one of his two meetings with Saddam Hussein, at which he had seemingly forgotten his recent(ish) description of the Iraqi government as a 'bestial dictatorship' and offered the man in charge the following tribute: 'Sir, I salute your courage, your strength, your indefatigability.' Any piece of writing involving Mr Galloway must tackle this most notorious of episodes, so here goes: in his telling of the tale, he had come to Iraq from Palestine, still emotionally reeling from a visit to the Occupied Territories, and had intended to pay homage to the spirit of the Iraqi people. Unfortunately, it came out slightly wrong. 'I should have known better,' he later claimed. 'I allowed my emotions to run away with me. I said things in a way I shouldn't have.'

Surveying Mr Galloway's history, one senses a life recurrently lived according to a slightly dangerous maxim: Why state your position cautiously when you can risk your entire political career with a melodramatic, unspeakably provocative soundbite that sounds like something from the last act of *Macbeth*? At the outbreak of the 2003 Iraq war, he did it again, when he told Abu-Dhabi TV that Bush and Blair had attacked Iraq 'like wolves', went on to query why Arab countries had not come to Iraq's aid, and advised any British soldiers watching that they were best off refusing to obey their 'illegal orders'. And so, about six months later, he was expelled from the Labour Party – though, in the manner of a spurned lover, he told me that he probably would have made the break anyway. 'I wish now that I had left the Labour Party,' he said, 'rather than waiting for them to kick me out.'

The following year came the launch of Respect, pledged to a string of righteously left-wing policies – 'No more British participation in US wars. No more bogus Trojan-horse "partnerships" with the private sector. An end to the witch-hunting of minorities, immigrants and asylum-seekers' – and named with one of those cart-before-the-horse acronyms. It had seemingly been chosen on account of its supposed streets-iness, and then accorded a chain of words that just about represented where Mr Galloway and his allies were coming from: Respect, Equality, Socialism, Peace, Environment, Community, Trade Unionism. As two minutes with a pen and a beermat proved, they could have been equally well served by WICKED (Workers' Iraq Coalition, also Kicking off on the Environment and Democracy) or SELECTA (Socialism, Environment, Left-wing Events, Collecting Tins And everything).

The party was born out of the march-organising Stop the War coalition, and thus initially founded on an unlikely alliance of Mr Galloway, the SWP and the Muslim Association of Britain. If the bond between the secular left and stringently fundamentalist Islam (according to an *Observer* article, the MAB believe that 'the punishment for Muslims who abandon their faith should be death') looked unlikely – not least when it came to matters of gay rights – Mr Galloway claimed that, for the moment, the accord was holding firm. Respect, according to its foundation statement, was pledged to support 'the right to self-determination of every individual in relation to their religious (or non-religious) beliefs, as well as sexual choices.' Thus far, he claimed, the only source of internal controversy had been his own opposition to abortion.

'The ultra-left press are going bananas about that,' he said. 'I did expect trouble to break out between the left part and the Muslim part of our coalition, but that hasn't happened. In fact, the Muslims signed up for our programme of self-determination in personal–political matters without demur. And, as I say, I'm the one getting it in the neck on those moral issues.' He grinned. 'But I can take it.'

So here they were, aiming to convince disaffected Labour voters that the war, the continued occupation of Iraq and the government's record on just about everything else meant that a vote for Mr Blair was inconceivable, not even the distant prospect of Gordon Brown entering 10 Downing Street would correct New Labour's crimes, and a protest vote for the Liberal Democrats actually represented no kind of protest at all.

'Charles Kennedy got out of bed on a Sunday morning a few weeks ago to appear on the David Frost programme and tell us, in case we were in any doubt, that the Liberal Democrats favoured the continuation of the occupation of Iraq,' said Mr Galloway. 'So, Kennedy, Howard and Blair are all for the same thing. Kennedy spoke at our February 15th demonstration, and then, as soon as the firing started, fell behind the utterly bogus notion that when war begins, one must support our boys. Well, only if you think "My country right or wrong" is a proper political philosophy. It's my view, shared by a lot of people, that if something is wrong before it's done, it's even more wrong *once* it's been done.

'So,' he continued, 'We're saying to people, it would be a better way of telling Mr Blair what you think to vote for an explicitly anti-war, explicitly anti-occupation and explicitly centre-left alternative. We'll be competing with the Liberal Democrats, I'll grant you that. And one of the places we're most keenly competing is among Muslim voters: 1.6 million of them. And I think we're winning that competition.'

In a far-off, dreamy future, Mr Galloway had his eyes fixed on a parliamentary bloc of sixty-five or so left-wing, non-Labour Party MPs. As far as the next General Election was concerned, Respect, with the aid of a strong base among local Muslims, were aiming at putting up candidates in fifty or sixty carefully-selected constituencies, taking aim at what Mr Galloway called – with another grandiloquent flourish – 'the worst of the war criminals, the worst of the betrayers'. The Labour MPs who had opposed the invasion of Iraq could rest easy, but those who had supported the enterprise could be expect to be the recipients of Respect's equivalent of Shock and Awe. 'Yesterday I was in Tower Hamlets,' he said. 'Tower Hamlets has a huge anti-war movement, and two pro-war MPs: Jim Fitzpatrick and Oona King. Under any conceivable circumstances, we will stand against both of those. We would never stand against people who were against the war – we wouldn't dream of standing in Hampstead against Glenda Jackson. But Jack Straw, in Blackburn, where there's a big anti-war movement, would be another one where it would be inconceivable for us not to stand. There will be other places. In Birmingham, for example.'

Among several misgivings about what Respect were up to, there were two things that particularly bothered me. The first was pretty straightforward, founded on the fears that the Labour Party so happily stokes. Like most left-wing challenges to Labour, Respect were perhaps fated to attract very little support at all, but – in some constituencies at least – siphon enough votes from Labour candidates that they might contribute to gains for the Tories. And where would that leave the put-upon multitudes for whom Respect aimed to speak?

'Well, there's a double answer to that,' said Mr Galloway. 'First of all, if we really are in a situation where Labour has an unprecedentedly massive majority, but no one can afford to vote against it from the left because you'll let the Tories in, that just shows what a disastrous job New Labour has done.'

I'm sure it does, I said. But it doesn't necessarily mean it won't happen.

'Well, to allow such a huge blunder as is implicit in your question to go unpunished, would be merely to encourage still more blunders,' he said. 'If people on the centre-left continue to vote for the New Labour project, however right-wing it becomes, why should it stop becoming right wing? If it's guaranteed the votes of centre-left people because they don't want Michael Howard in, why should it stop where it's stopped? Why shouldn't it march endlessly into wars and more and more privatisation? Unless centre-left people make a stand, there will be *no* centre-left. And one of the ways of making a stand is by supporting a credible centre-left alternative. And that's what I hope we will become.'

My second problem was, somewhat inevitably, bound up with some of the political company Mr Galloway was keeping – specifically, the Socialist Workers Party. When he talked about the 'centre-left', could he really include the kind of non-compromising, fundamentalist, cliquey political simpletons who were once labelled 'Trots'?

'Mmmmm,' said Mr Galloway, wearily.

I don't like Trots at all, I said. And I know that you don't, from reading your book.

'No, I don't,' he said. 'I have a long track record of opposition to them.'

Then what, I wondered, was he doing in an alliance with them?

'Well,' he said. 'I think, first of all, in this post-Soviet world, we have to redefine our terms. We're no longer really talking about Trots. What we're really talking about is ultra-leftism. If we come across ultra-left groups, we certainly know about it. And the SWP doesn't behave in an ultra-left way. If it did, it wouldn't have been the driving force behind the Stop the War movement, which brought two million people onto the streets. Millions of people have been engaged in that movement – and if the SWP had run the Stop the War coalition in an ultra-left way, that would not have been possible. There aren't two million Trotskyists in Britain.

'Like everyone else, they're changing,' he assured me. 'Their leaders are changing. Old ideas are seen to have failed, new ones come along. I think what you've got now is an SWP that wants to work in a broad way. I think they've taken a parliamentary road; so you should rejoice, rejoice, and not be churlish about it.'

The following week, by way of checking on Mr Galloway's claims, I bought a copy of *Socialist Worker*. It did not exactly fill me with good cheer. It took only the most casual flick-through before I alighted on exactly the kind of stiff, archaic prose that always makes the far-left sound like some secular version of the Jehovah's Witnesses.

Today, the working class is the largest class in the world. No previous exploited class had the organising capacity of modern workers. Concentrated in vast cities, in great productive enterprises, workers have the means to organise themselves on a huge scale. The organised working class offers the single most important arena for socialist activity. Trade Unions are especially important. They are the frontline organisations in the class struggle.

I also thought I'd go to one of the public meetings organised by Respect to assist their campaign effort for 2004's Euro elections. It happened in early June at the Lighthouse Arts Centre in Wolverhampton, where two of the party's other stars were scheduled to make an appearance: John Rees, a senior member of the SWP, one of the public faces of the Stop the War coalition, and a Respect Euro-candidate for the West Midlands; and Yvonne Ridley, the sometime *Sunday Express* foreign correspondent who was fleetingly kidnapped by the Taliban, only to return to the UK, convert to Islam, and decide to run as a Respect candidate in the North East.

At around the meeting's scheduled kick-off, one of Respect's local activists uttered a sentence I had not heard since the mid-80s: 'We'll give it ten more minutes and then get going.' The imagined droves united by slow-running watches failed to swell the numbers; so it was that a panel of four faced an audience of about twenty-five, most of whom seemed to know one another. In that context, it was perhaps unfortunate that Yvonne Ridley decided to stick rigidly to a speech obviously prepared in a spirit of misplaced optimism. 'We are the largest mass political movement this country has ever seen,' she said, alluding to Respect's origins in February 2003's Hyde Park march. She sounded a bit like one of those dreamy musicians who take the stage at thinly populated pub backrooms but feel duty-bound to yelp 'Hello London!'

After Ms Ridley had finished by claiming that Tony Blair was 'dripping with the blood of Palestinian children' – which was nice – she made way for Phil Goldby, a local convenor for the Fire Brigades Union. Then came John Rees, who had a David Brent beard and a slightly raffish, swept-back haircut, and glad tidings to dispense. 'This is a government in very deep crisis,' he said. 'Tony Blair's resignation is only a step away.' After capably skipping through Abu Ghraib, the Lib Dems' endless sell-outs, the restoration of the link between earnings and pensions and the dreadful state of the railways, he arrived at his tub-thumping conclusion: 'We have a chance, now, to turn the political tide, to change the nature of protest and how it's expressed within the system.' The audience clapped with all the enthusiasm they could muster.

Then came questions from the floor. To audible groans, a bearded, bespectacled man – a representative of Wolverhampton Trades Union Council, he said – rose to his feet and asked what Respect thought they were doing, attempting to draw votes away from the Labour Party and thus (as he saw it, anyway) increasing the possibility of gains for the British National Party. John Rees testily told him that his analysis was based on a mistaken understanding of how Euro elections actually work, but that failed to end the argument. 'Besides all that,' said his adversary, 'what everyone should know is that Respect is just a front for the SWP.'

'He's a fucking *Morning Star* Communist,' someone muttered. Given my absence from the coalface of far-left debate for the last eighteen years, I wasn't quite sure exactly what this meant, but it seemed to amount to something very bad.

Soon after, a middle-aged, unremarkable-looking man – who remained seated – asked an innocent-sounding question about someone called Steve Godward, who was apparently standing as an 'Independent Firefighter' in council elections in the Erdington area of Birmingham. Why, he asked, hadn't Mr Godward received a Respect endorsement?

John Rees, who had spent his time on his feet addressing the most pressing political issues facing both the UK and the wider world, seemed only too happy to leap into the local undergrowth. 'Well,' he said, 'I would really have a problem supporting Steve Godward because of his stance on the war in Iraq.'

There was an awkward silence. 'I know Steve personally,' said the unremarkable-looking man. 'And believe me: he really does oppose the war.'

In Baghdad, bullets were doubtless ricocheting off city walls, while the nightshift clocked on at Abu Ghraib and children walked on the remains of cluster bombs. For now, it mattered not.

'If that's true,' said John Rees. 'Steve should put his views in his literature. Then these problems wouldn't arise.'

'Well, I'll pass that on,' said the unremarkable-looking man, with a brittle sense of defeat.

When the meeting was declared over, he ran outside and stood stoically with a batch of a newspaper called *Workers' Power*, the journal of 'the British Section of the League for the Fifth International' (who, I discovered after buying a copy, reckoned that Respect represented 'a diversion from the struggle for socialism'). In the foyer, the bloke from Wolverhampton Trades Union Council was loudly swearing at a gaggle of Respect activists, before he and two friends shouted their last and went to the pub to discuss the night's events and engage in the traditional left-wing ritual my grandfather used to call 'lining the pockets of the Tory brewers'.

Later that week came the Euro elections. For all my scepticism, I was slightly pained by just how dismally Respect performed. In the North East, Yvonne Ridley came pretty much bottom, finishing with 1.11 per cent of the vote. In Wales, things were yet worse: Respect managed a microscopic 0.59 per cent. Even in the West Midlands, where the power of the Muslim vote had been so frantically talked up, John Rees received only 2.41 per cent, finishing a mere 0.8 of a point above the little-known Pensioners Party. Only in London did they manage something close to – arf, arf – respectability: reportedly thanks to a strong showing in what used to be known as the East End, George Galloway amassed 91,175 votes, 4.84 per cent of the total but a mere 0.8 of a point more than the BNP.

These were early days, admittedly. Mr Galloway and his friends would doubtless pin much of the blame on a hostile press, a broadcasting media that failed to give them much coverage, and – who knows? – the delusional consciousness that arises as a result of capitalist relations of production. Somewhere within the rhetorical melodrama and saloon-bar sectarian warfare I'd seen in Wolverhampton, however, there lurked an altogether more crushing explanation. Perhaps, as ever, the far-left had no one to blame but themselves.

6 So now who do we vote for?

Back in the 1980s, when I so happily signed my Labour Party membership papers, arriving at a feeling of political certainty was wonderfully easy. The Tories, naturally, were an utterly evil force, intent on dismantling just about everything for which our side had ever fought. The Liberal Democrats, in those days split into the Liberals and treacherous SDP, were deluded fools who had divided the progressive vote and thus handed the Conservatives power (an argument that rather ignored the mess our party was in, though it seemed convincing enough). The far left, as anti-Trot partisans like me well knew, amounted to a shower of unpleasant fantasists who had long since lost sight of the real enemy. The Labour Party, however, was – cue trumpets, ticker tape, and Billy Bragg leading a women-only choir into a chorus of the Red Flag – our one true hope, rooted in a long and proud history, and eventually destined to roll back the Thatcherite tide. Such was the basis of those long, anti-climactic evenings spent either posting leaflets through letterboxes or debating motions that instantly slipped into irrelevance.

During my work on this book, I was recurrently struck by how much the two decades since had mired all that in doubt (aside from the bit concerning the Tories, obviously). The result was the queasy feeling that comes from being cut adrift – but there again, part of me also felt newly liberated. Where once I had displayed all the symptoms of political addiction, that side of my mind was now open – and if 2001 had found previously staunch Labour supporters like me at least thinking about taking our votes somewhere else, the next election offered the prospect of a decision based on rational grounds. Just imagine: more than five seconds in the voting booth, no thick-headed fixation with the box marked 'Labour' – *choice*, as Mr Blair would have it.

In that sense, it was hardly surprising that the interviews aimed at answering this book's central question found me buffeted from one tentative solution to another. Though meeting Charles Kennedy had me ranting to my friends about his apparent uselessness, two hours with Lembit Öpik left me wishing all Liberal Democrats were like that, so I could confidently jump ship. Just as my old suspicions of the Lib Dems could occasionally come close to melting away, so hostility to the extremist headbangers of yore was at least momentarily sidelined: though the Respect Coalition is a rum old organisation, I will admit that, if only on account of its upturn-the-Monopoly-board air of last-ditch fury, I was initially quite taken with the idea of a newly energised challenge to Mr Blair from the far left. Stranger still, my empathy with Plaid Cymru's Simon Thomas (in tandem with the fact that I had just moved to Wales) led me to fleetingly consider joining them, before I concluded that – doh! – my indifference to the argument for Welsh independence probably ruled me out.

All that said, and though I no longer suffer from the political myopia of twenty years ago, I would still *like* to vote Labour. Some of this residual loyalty, I cannot deny, is down to fairly idiotic emotionalism, tied to the stuff of history – but I can also make a rational(ish) case for it. For a start, more than just about all the other politicians I encountered, the three senior party dissidents I met gave me the same sense of common cause that defined my time in the party all those years ago. Second, the fact that Blair's second term has seen large-scale parliamentary rebellions – on the war in Iraq, top-up fees and Foundation Hospitals – proves that their kind of thinking has not yet been extinguished. I'm not sure one can use a word like 'despite' in the context of this government's endless transgressions – but despite Iraq, and PFI, and their plans for the effective break-up of the NHS, and the marketisation of higher education, and City Academies and LEA outsourcing, and the return of Alan Milburn to the Cabinet . . . a large part of me cannot argue with Roy Hattersley's claim that 'the idea of equality will remain. And the Labour Party is the best possible vehicle for it'.

Where we differ is on the circumstances in which both idea and party might be revived. Even in the context of Blair's promised retirement, I don't see that a return to a position somewhere to his left is inevitable, or that the agenda he has pursued is necessarily some passing aberration that will soon wither. Moreover, if the sloughing-off of the Blairite project will supposedly be the work of the party outside Parliament, there are grounds for real pessimism. On the few occasions when I have gone back to have a look, it has frequently seemed so shrivelled as to be incapable of asserting its will. In 2001, for example, I found myself wandering around the outer rings of the annual party conference, desperate to catch a glimpse of that day's proceedings. All I could find was a bank of TVs showing a timid question-and-answer session with Alan Milburn and Estelle Morris, which looked like an edition of *This Morning* given over to the kind of subjects you read about in *Society Guardian*. I asked a passing union official where I might be able to view the proceedings of conference. 'That is conference,' he said.

The best we can hope for, it often seems, is New Labour shorn of some of its more unacceptable aspects. PFI will remain; tuition fees too, in all likelihood. Those of us who believe that left-leaning politics will never make much headway without a drive to address the UK's resistance to more progressive taxation will be disappointed. But some things might go: slavish obeisance to American foreign policy, no matter how reckless; the idea that schools and hospitals are best improved by setting them against one another; a premium placed on the 'choice' that can be exercised by the privileged, while the less fortunate are left with only the scraps.

If at least some of that is to happen, the prescription offered by the ex-minister in Chapter Three seems unarguable: 'For the sake of Labour's values and the future of the party, a correction has to take place . . . The party needs a fright.' If we are talking here, in crudely reductive terms, about a Gordon Brown premiership, then it also might be an idea if it was the right kind of Gordon Brown premiership: one based on the need for Labour to renew itself, and reconnect to its traditions. There is only one way this will be achieved: by the party realising that much of its core support, albeit temporarily, has gone somewhere else.

That scenario raises another, slightly more far-off prospect. These days, British politics often seems to revolve around the desperate pursuit of the floating voters whose default position is support for the Tories – the people who, to all intents and purposes, form New Labour's foundation stone. The spectacle of equal numbers of disaffected progressives suddenly revealing that their votes were up for grabs could conceivably nudge the political centre leftwards, and allow for the kind of ideas that pepper this book to rise to the surface. Initially at least, this will be more a matter of backbench rhetoric than government policy, but it might be a start.

As things stand, 'ideological' has mutated into the worst kind of political insult, and political debate is very rarely bound up with competing views of the best kind of society. Woolly politics begets woolly rhetoric: an endless cacophony in which all our politicians babble about freedom, fairness and justice, and occasionally attempt to edge the debate forward with buzz-phrases – New Localism, The Personalisation of Public Services – that make precious little sense outside SW1. In February 2004, for example, the Tories attempted to steal the headlines being accorded to Labour's 'Big Conversation' by hailing the new concept of 'The British Dream'. Really: who cares?

Out in the real world, however, the lines of battle seem as sharp as ever. 'Which side are you on?' is the kind of question that seems rooted in a long-gone era, but when I visited the Cumberland Infirmary, or the headquarters of the Bradford NUT, or the community centre from which Tracy Morton and Kay Wilkinson were fighting the arrival of a Vardy Academy, I met people with the same sense of first-principle outrage that used to course around our veins in the 1980s. Whenever the government outlines its plans for a sparkling new NHS, I think of Linda Weightman, the scrubs-nurse-turned-union-convenor I met in Carlisle. 'You ask the staff in this hospital and they'll tell you,' she said. 'It's *immoral* to make money out of people who are ill.'

If service companies are allowed to carry on eating into our public services, corporate power continues to exert a strangulating influence on our towns and cities, and government frequently pays greater heed to private finance than the public interest, those kind of voices will only grow louder. If they don't find a place in the mainstream, our politics seems set for further decay.

At the 2001 election, one of the more disquieting consequences of Mr Blair's time in government became clear: turnout dropped to 59.4 per cent, at least partly on account of alienated Labour supporters remaining at home. Current forecasts suggest that at the next election, things will get worse; certainly, if dismay in Labour's heartlands is an even bigger factor, the predictions will be proved right.

I have friends who talk about not voting with a backhanded kind of pride, as if it represents the very acme of radicalism; some of them, moreover, have occasionally come up with a theory that sitting on one's hands might result in politics being restored to health, as our MPs realise that half the population has switched off and belatedly attempt to re-root the Westminster ritual in our everyday lives. The progressive case, however, has little to gain from abstention: it surely represents the kind of indecipherable protest that the powerful inevitably re-interpret for their own ends. Thus far, when ministers have publicly fretted about a disconnection from politics, they have tended to do so in the context of a need to address such issues as crime, asylum and immigration; it's impossible to imagine a low turnout in 2005 somehow propelling politics to the left. Voting, then, is pretty much imperative – as is using one's ballot paper to maximum effect.

Our creaking electoral system – more of which later – is particularly cruel to anyone wanting to vote against the Labour Party from the left. You might resolve to jump one way; simultaneously, droves of *Daily Mail* readers may well leap in the other direction, rendering your gesture of protest irrelevant and allowing your constituency to be hailed as a new bastion of Howard-ism: the sort of place where people care chiefly about low taxes, the death of the pound and rampant hooligans. This, of course, is the nub of all those government howls about sticking with Mr Blair, lest the country fall into the abyss.

One's instinctive response might be to tut, and vote against the government anyway: if the summation of a hundred years of Labour history is simply 'Vote for us, or you'll get the Tories', then Mr Blair and his friends may be hardly worthy of even grudging support. Nonetheless, this book does not advocate the electoral equivalent of strapping dynamite to your chest: righteously voting against the Labour Party in whatever circumstances, with a blithe indifference to the consequences. I can't agree with the ex-minister's argument that a government led by Michael Howard might not be much worse than a third Blair administration: if the market-driven, authoritarian ways of New Labour seem repulsive, the Tories' insatiable enthusiasm for both privatisation and the illiberal use of state power make them even more toxic. The first may be unpalatable; the second is unthinkable. Imagine the morning after a Tory victory, and just how glib all those claims of political equivalence would suddenly sound.

Mercifully, at the time of writing, a Conservative triumph at the next election seems so unlikely as to appear laughable. To form the government, the Tories would have to take back seats in the places that decisively closed their doors to them in 1997; just as Neil Kinnock never had any hope of re-establishing Labour in the Home Counties, so Michael Howard must know that Scotland, Wales and the larger English cities will not deliver the boost he needs to enter Downing Street. Moreover, there are plenty of seats where the choice on offer goes beyond two-party politics.

When asked about tactical voting, one of the politicians interviewed in this book offered the opinion that it amounts to 'a rough and ready form of proportional representation: you're skipping your first preference and going straight to the second.' He has an undeniable point, and with that in mind, one can start to arrive at a kind of strategy.

In short, your local circumstances are everything. First, as mentioned above, if you share the kind of beliefs that pervade this book, there are a large number of Labour MPs who still deserve your support, on account of their opposition to the government on Iraq, Foundation Hospitals and tuition fees (their names are listed in the appendix). A vote against the war may be enough to put them out of harm's way; within the same roll-call, however, are several people who took the quixotic decision to oppose the government's plans for the NHS and/or higher education, having already trooped through the lobbies to back the Prime Minister's rush to armed conflict, surely his most objectionable enterprise to date. Maybe guilt belatedly converted them to the rebel cause; all that can perhaps be said with confidence is that these strange souls shouldn't be viewed with quite the disdain heaped on robotically loyal Blairites.

In Labour/Tory marginals, things will inevitably be rather complicated. (To check how close the parties were running at the last General Election, visit www.electoralcommission.org. uk.) Even if the Conservatives mount the most inept challenge to the government, it seems certain that a few more of the Tories who switched to Labour in 1997 and began to trickle back in 2001 will decide to return home, which puts a slew of Labour seats in a perilous position. A few names illustrate the point: in such constituencies as Milton Keynes North East, Braintree, Kettering and Shipley, voting Labour may be truly painful – horrific, even – but it will probably be obligatory. Even where the gap between the two main parties is a little wider, you might have to think hard – and in places where Labour is running a very close second to the Tories, electoral logic might dictate a counter-intuitive vote for them. In places like these, what Roy Hattersley so sternly told me makes inescapable sense: the race really is between Tony Blair and Michael Howard.

Elsewhere, however, the choices are slightly easier. As has been said a few times in the preceding pages, the Liberal Democrats' opposition to the invasion of Iraq may have been lamentably hesitant, and their positions on the public services worryingly indistinguishable from New Labour's (their 2004 'pre-manifesto', for example, failed to mention PFI or Foundation Hospitals), but they remain a viable refuge for dismayed Labour supporters. For all their shortcomings, they're the most high-profile receptacle for anti-war protest, and their stances on tuition fees, long-term care for the elderly, and a higher top rate of tax only strengthen their position. In that sense, one's chief option in the small number of Labour/Liberal Democrat marginals – like Oldham East and Saddleworth, Rochdale and Birmingham Yardley – shouldn't be too hard to work out, as is the case in the relatively large number of constituencies where the Lib Dems are either in control or challenging the Tories (who, let us not forget, are almost as deserving of Iraq-based protest voting as the Labour Party).

There will also be a clutch of inner-city, multi-racial seats where the Lib Dems are likely to claim that anti-war opinion will allow them to leapfrog the Tories and mount a challenge to Labour from third place; the Respect Coalition won't like it, but if the results of the Brent East and Leicester South by-elections are anything to go by, they may well have a point. In all these cases, the Lib Dems' drawbacks are an irritant, but surely offset by the potential pleasure of watching the country's political pundits come to the inescapable conclusion that Liberal Democrat successes are chiefly emblematic of both undimmed opposition to the war and anger at Mr Blair's disregard for the conventions of democracy.

Across Labour's heartlands, meanwhile, there are a multitude of seats in which the party's share of the vote far exceeds 50 per cent, leaving their opponents fighting for electoral crumbs. There are masses of these constituencies in Scotland and Wales, along with such English Labour heartlands as South Yorkshire, Liverpool, Manchester and inner London. Here, of all places, the Blairites deserve a jolt: the New Labour project, after all, is based on the calculation that while waverers in the marginals are zealously pursued, these seats can be taken for granted. As I came to suspect while hearing the story of the proposed Vardy Academy in Conisbrough, that has often made them safe for some of New Labour's most noxious experiments – can you imagine an evangelical car dealer being handed the control of a state school in Basildon or Swindon?

Whether you vote Liberal Democrat, Green, Respect, Plaid Cymru or SNP, one thing seems certain: Labour's grip on these constituencies needs to be loosened if the party is ever to leave the Blair era behind. The MPs who represent such places include droves of New Labour zealots – not least the Prime Minister himself, sitting atop a 64.9 per cent share of the vote in Sedgefield – which surely only increases the necessity of voting against them. These are the people who need the wake-up call; thankfully, it can be delivered without fear of handing any accidental fillip to the Tories.

And then there are the seats whose battles are built on national and local peculiarities. The Greens' position in Brighton Pavilion probably isn't quite as strong as they suggest, but the fact that they might even come second holds out the promise of a quiet shake-up of the usual political certainties. The Respect Coalition's performance at last year's Euro elections might suggest something close to irrelevance – but their showing in East London was strong enough to suggest that their pledge to take on such pro-war MPs as Oona King and Jim Fitzpatrick might just be worthy of being taken seriously. In Scotland, the SNP will fix its attentions on a few Labour marginals; in Wales, Plaid Cymru's main hope is the constituency of Ynys Mon – though the rebellious voting record of its sitting Labour MP slightly weakens their case.

One final point needs restating. Those who are used to voting Labour might find all kinds of drawbacks with the parties mentioned above. The Liberal Democrats couple their timidity with occasional shuffling to the right; Plaid Cymru and the SNP are both founded on a goal that may well arouse either indifference or hostility; the Greens are prone to seem both muddled and naive, and Respect are tainted by fundamentalism, both political and religious. All of them, however, oppose the government on at least some of the right issues, and hold out the prospect of the delivery of a shock. For one election at least, that's surely enough.

*

In June last year, the venerable Tony Benn was asked how he would vote in the forthcoming European and local elections. He stressed his loyalty to a Labour Party he claimed had been hijacked, before offering an opinion that cut to the political quick. 'New Labour doesn't have any support,' he said. 'You can't imagine canvassing and people saying, "Oh yes, I'm New Labour, I'd like to privatise the Post Office, I'd like to have more loans for students and, oh yes, let's have another war."'

In 2001, Labour won 42 per cent of the vote, a smaller proportion than that managed by any post-war government apart from the Harold Wilson administration of the mid-70s. Given that year's lamentable turnout, the figure actually represented around a quarter of eligible voters – and yet Labour's senior figures talked in terms of a ringing popular endorsement. If that seems absurd, consider the calculation that lies at the heart of their stern warning to those who might desert the party at the next election: by voting for anyone other than Labour, you allegedly put the country at risk of majority government by the Tories – who, similarly, won't be supported by much more than 25 per cent of the electorate.

Reform of the voting system is not exactly the most glamorous of political issues. Though the people who became the Liberal Democrats spent much of the 1980s attempting to push it to the centre of the debate – older readers might remember party political broadcasts in which John Cleese stood in front of a blackboard, passionately outlining the benefits of proportional representation – they eventually nudged the issue into the middle distance (in 2001, it sat towards the back of their manifesto, one page on from a section entitled 'Business, Innovation and

Consumers'). The early days of the Blair government, when a commission headed by Roy Jenkins came up with a modest proposal for the so-called 'alternative vote top-up system', saw the hopes of reformers momentarily raised, though nothing has been heard of it since. Back then, the Labour Party tapped into its long-standing antipathy towards the Lib Dems and ruled the idea out; as with most governments, New Labour's addiction to unrivalled power has ensured that it has continued to keep such dangerous ideas at arm's length.

Away from Westminster, however, the benefits of PR are obvious. The political landscapes of Scotland and Wales are at least partly traceable to the fact that the views of those who sit to the left of the modern Labour Party actually count; the same applies, on a much more modest level, to the European Parliament and London Assembly, and the platform accorded to the Greens. If one of the more bizarre effects of the first-past-the-post system is a politics tied to Tory-leaning swing voters, PR for Westminster could be reasonably expected to open things up. On account of new threats from the left, the Labour Party would be forced to pay attention to the people who form its electoral bedrock; on the current figures, it could only form a majority government with the assistance of the Lib Dems. In the distant past, Labour supporters might have fretted about such a scenario compromising the party's socialism – these days, as proved by the coalition that rules in Scotland, it might actually lead to the odd decision that left-leaning people would applaud.

As things stand, we march against war, froth about the iniquities of tuition fees and Foundation Hospitals, loudly bemoan the privatisation of our public services – and then wonder where the seemingly unstoppable momentum behind it all might have originated. At least part of the answer might lie in an electoral system that has turned hideously dysfunctional.

It sounds ever-so-slightly fanciful, but it's worth saying: if votes were finally reflected in seats, the anti-war, pro-public sector, progressive voters recurrently ignored by our politicians might actually exercise a powerful influence on government. Can you *imagine*?

APPENDIX Labour Rebels

The following Labour MPs, along with some who have been omitted because they are known to be standing down at the next election, voted against the government on the war in Iraq, Foundation Hospitals and tuition fees. In all three cases, there were at least two salient votes. On Iraq, February 2003 saw voting on an amendment advocating the resolution of the issue via the UN, but the crucial decision took place that March, when – on the eve of war – MPs voted on an amendment claiming that there was no moral case for an attack. On Foundation Hospitals, the decision came to the wire in November 2003 with a Commons vote on an anti-Foundation Hospitals amendment proposed by the House of Lords; when it came to top-up fees, the interim between the legislation's second and third reading by the Commons saw some rebels converted to the government's argument. In all three cases, the decisions indicated (by I, FH and TF) related to the later of the votes on each issue. They have been selected not only for the sake of simplicity, but also to highlight MPs who held their nerve. For a more detailed breakdown of individual MPs' voting behaviour, it's a good idea to use the *Guardian*'s Ask Aristotle Service at www.guardian.co.uk/politics. A very enlightening list of the Labour MPs who voted for the Iraq war, along with their constituency majorities, is at www.eurolegal.org/british/prowarlabmp.htm.

Diane Abbott, Hackney North & Stoke Newington (I, FH, TF)
Graham Allen, Nottingham North (I)
John Austin, Erith & Thamesmead (I, FH)
Tony Banks, West Ham (I)
Harry Barnes, Derbyshire North East (I, FH, TF)
John Battle, Leeds West (I)
Andrew Bennett, Denton & Reddish (I, FH)
Joe Benton, Bootle (I)
Roger Berry, Kingswood (I, FH, TF)
Harold Best, Leeds North West (I, FH)
Bob Blizzard, Waveney (I)
Keith Bradley, Manchester Withington (I)
Kevin Brennan, Cardiff West (I)
Karen Buck, Regent's Park & Kensington North (I)
Richard Burden, Birmingham Northfield (I)
Colin Burgon, Elmet (FH, TF)
Anne Campbell, Cambridge (I)
Ronnie Campbell, Blyth Valley (I)
Martin Caton, Gower (I, FH, TF)
David Chaytor, Bury North (I)
Michael Clapham, Barnsley West & Penistone (I, FH, TF)
Helen Clark, Peterborough (I, TF)
Tom Clarke, Coatbridge & Chryston (I)
Tony Clarke, Northampton South (I, FH)
Harry Cohen, Leyton & Wanstead (I)
Iain Coleman, Hammersmith & Fulham (I, FH)
Tony Colman, Putney (TF)
Michael Connarty, Falkirk East (I)
Frank Cook, Stockton North (I, FH)
Robin Cook, Livingston (I)
Jeremy Corbyn, Islington North (I, FH, TF)
Jim Cousins, Newcastle upon Tyne Central (I)
Tom Cox, Tooting (I)
David Crausby, Bolton North East (I, TF)
Jon Cruddas, Dagenham (TF)

Ann Cryer, Keighley (I)
John Cryer, Hornchurch (I)
Valerie Davey, Bristol West (I)
Ian Davidson, Glasgow Pollok (I, FH, TF)
Denzil Davies, Llanelli (I)
Hilton Dawson, Lancaster & Wyre (I)
John Denham, Southampton Itchen (I)
Parmjit Dhanda, Gloucester (I)
Andrew Dismore, Hendon (TF)
Jim Dobbin, Heywood & Middleton (I, FH, TF)
Frank Dobson, Holborn & St Pancras (I, FH, TF)
Frank Doran, Aberdeen Central (I)
David Drew, Stroud (I)
Julia Drown, Swindon South (FH)
Gwyneth Dunwoody, Crewe & Nantwich (FH, TF)
Huw Edwards, Monmouth (I)
Clive Efford, Eltham (I, FH)
Jeff Ennis, Barnsley East & Mexborough (TF)
Bill Etherington, Sunderland North (I)
Frank Field, Birkenhead (FH)
Mark Fisher, Stoke-on-Trent Central (I, FH, TF)
Paul Flynn, Newport West (I, FH)
Hywel Francis, Aberavon (I)
Neil Gerrard, Walthamstow (I, FH)
Ian Gibson, Norwich North (I, FH, TF)
Roger Godsiff, Birmingham Sparkbrook & Small Heath (I, FH, TF)
Win Griffiths, Bridgend (I)
John Grogan, Selby (I, TF)
Patrick Hall, Bedford (I)
David Hamilton, Midlothian (I)
Fabian Hamilton, Leeds North East (I)
Dai Havard, Merthyr Tydfil & Rhymney (I, FH, TF)
Doug Henderson, Newcastle upon Tyne North (I, FH)
Stephen Hepburn, Jarrow (I)
David Heyes, Ashton under Lyne (I)

David Hinchliffe, Wakefield (I, FH)

Kate Hoey, Vauxhall (I, FH, TF)

Jimmy Hood, Clydesdale (I)

Kelvin Hopkins, Luton North (I, FH)

Lindsay Hoyle, Chorley (TF)

Joan Humble, Blackpool North & Fleetwood (I)

Alan Hurst, Braintree (TF)

Brian Iddon, Bolton South East (I, TF)

Eric Illsley, Barnsley Central (I, FH, TF)

Glenda Jackson, Hampstead & Highgate (I, FH, TF)

Helen Jackson, Sheffield Hillsborough (I)

Helen Jones, Warrington North (FH, TF)

Jon Owen Jones, Cardiff Central (I, TF)

Kevan Jones, Durham North (FH)

Lynne Jones, Birmingham Selly Oak (I, FH, TF)

Martyn Jones, Clwyd South (I)

David Kidney, Stafford (I)

Peter Kilfoyle, Liverpool Walton (I, FH, TF)

Andy King, Rugby & Kenilworth (FH)

Mark Lazarowicz, Edinburgh North & Leith (I)

David Lepper, Brighton Pavilion (I)

Terry Lewis, Worsley (I, TF)

Tony Lloyd, Manchester Central (I, FH, TF)

Ian Lucas, Wrexham (I)

Iain Luke, Dundee East (I)

John Lyons, Strathkelvin & Bearsden (I)

Christine McCafferty, Calder Valley (I, FH, TF)

John McDonnell, Hayes & Harlington (I, FH, TF)

Ann McKechin, Glasgow Maryhill (I)

Kevin McNamara, Hull North (I, TF)

Tony McWalter, Hemel Hempstead (I)

Bob Marshall-Andrews, Medway (I, FH, TF)

Eric Martlew, Carlisle (I)

Julie Morgan, Cardiff North (I, TF)

George Mudie, Leeds East (FH, TF)

Chris Mullin, Sunderland South (I)

Denis Murphy, Wansbeck (I)

Doug Naysmith, Bristol North West (I, FH)

Eddie O'Hara, Knowsley South (I)

Diana Organ, Forest of Dean (I)

Albert Owen, Ynys Mon (I, FH, TF)

Linda Perham, Ilford North (I)

Anne Picking, East Lothian (FH)

Peter Pike, Burnley (I)

Kerry Pollard, St Albans (I)

Gordon Prentice, Pendle (I, FH, TF)

Gwyn Prosser, Dover (I)

Ken Purchase, Wolverhampton North East (I, FH)

Joyce Quin, Gateshead East & Washington West (FH)

John Robertson, Glasgow Anniesland (I)

Joan Ruddock, Lewisham Deptford (I)

Martin Salter, Reading West (I)

Mohammed Sarwar, Glasgow Govan (I)

Malcolm Savidge, Aberdeen North (I)

Philip Sawford, Kettering (I)

Brian Sedgemore, Hackney South & Shoreditch (I, FH, TF)

Debra Shipley, Stourbridge (I)

Clare Short, Birmingham Ladywood (FH, TF)*

Alan Simpson, Nottingham South (I, FH, TF)

Marsha Singh, Bradford West (I)

Dennis Skinner (FH, TF)**

Chris Smith, Islington South & Finsbury (I)

Gerry Steinberg, City Of Durham (FH, TF)

George Stevenson, Stoke-on-Trent South (I, FH)

Gavin Strang, Edinburgh East & Musselburgh (I)

Graham Stringer, Manchester Blackley (I)

David Taylor, Leicestershire North West (I, FH, TF)

Jon Trickett, Hemsworth (I, FH, TF)

Paul Truswell, Pudsey (I)

Desmond Turner, Brighton Kemptown (I, FH)

Bill Tynan, Hamilton South (I)
Rudi Vis, Finchley & Golders Green (I)
Joan Walley, Stoke-on-Trent North (I, FH)
Robert Wareing, Liverpool West Derby (I, FH, TF)
Alan Whitehead, Southampton Test (I)
Alan Williams, Swansea West (I)
Betty Williams, Conwy (I)
Mike Wood, Batley & Spen (I, FH, TF)
David Wright, Telford (I)
Derek Wyatt, Sittingbourne & Sheppey (I)

* At the time of the two votes on Iraq, Clare Short was a member of the government. Inevitably, she voted with them on both occasions.
** Skinner voted with the rebels on the pro-UN amendment. When I phoned him to ask about his absence for the second Iraq vote, he said this: 'That's because I was lying in the Brompton Hospital having heart surgery. I voted against bombing Iraq when Mr Almighty Bloody Pure Virgin Robin Cook was the Foreign Secretary.'

Acknowledgements

Firstly, infinite credit goes to Hannah Griffiths of Faber and Faber, whose judgement, energy, powers of invention and motivational brilliance allowed a great deal of this book to feel like a collaborative enterprise. I am lucky not only to have her as an editor and friend, but to work with someone who has (1) amazing belief and (2) such a fantastic array of talents. Thanks also to my superb agent, Jonny Geller at Curtis Brown, and to Faber's other stars, particularly Anna Pallai and Charles Boyle.

Thanks to everyone who agreed to be interviewed, along with their assistants and aides, and to a couple of people whose contribution was more a matter of fantastically useful information: Martin Bell, and Allyson Pollock at UCL, whose book *NHS Plc: The Privatisation of Our Healthcare* (Verso) is recommended to anyone wishing to read more about the subjects examined in Chapter Two. I benefited from the direct help offered by Olive Forsythe at the NUT, and the work of David Butler and Dennis Kavanagh, whose series of British General Election books proved indispensable.

I'd also like to belatedly thank the people with whom I once shared evenings arguing over resolutions and persuading the public to vote Labour: Rod Pickford, Lucy Shorrocks, Jane Ryder, Jon Kelly, Deric Shaw, the late Doug Emerson – and the inestimable Neil Smith, with whom I agitated back in the 80s, and have shared many political epiphanies and passionate debates ever since. My largest debt on this score is to my dad, whose endless insights underpin a lot of the book, and who provided a reliable sounding board at particularly difficult moments; and my mum, who will – I hope, anyway – recognise her huge influence on the preceding pages.

Special thanks should also go to Hywel Harris, a true friend and ingenious creative partner (for more details, visit www.hywel.biz) who plunged into work on this book's accompanying website with both wisdom and vigour; Adam Smith, whose razor-like intellect has recurrently kept me on my toes for fifteen years; Colleen Harris and Aidan Bruce; Steve Lowe; Mark Lawson; Louise Wener and Andy Maclure; and Karl Rhys, who knows that if a door is closed, you should always open it. My biggest thanks, however, go to Ginny Luckhurst, for her love, patience, encouragement and sure grasp of the importance of home. Without her, I couldn't have even got started.

Given the subject of this book, I'll close by expressing fervent appreciation to Linda Weightman, Linda Devlin and Ron Dawson from the Carlisle branch of Unison, the Bradford NUT's Ian Murch and Jane Rendell, and Tracy Morton and Kay Wilkinson, founders of the Conisbrough and Denaby Parents' Action Group – all of whom not only gave me their time, but also proved that in the real world, what many take as a given is still being fiercely contested. They were by far the most inspiring people I met while writing and researching this book, and their example served to power me to the end.

John Harris

Hay on Wye, 2004